Kent Stories of the Supernatural

W. H. Johnson

COUNTRYSIDE BOOKS
NEWBURY, BERKSHIRE

First published 2000
© W. H. Johnson 2000

COUNTRYSIDE BOOKS
3 Catherine Road
Newbury, Berkshire

To view our complete range of books,
please visit us at
www.countrysidebooks.co.uk

ISBN 1 85306 650 8

Designed by Graham Whiteman
Cover painting by Colin Doggett

Produced through MRM Associates Ltd., Reading
Printed by J. W. Arrowsmith Ltd., Bristol

Contents

Acknowledgements

It is my hope that all of those who have helped me with this book will find their labours to have been worthwhile. I am conscious of the debt I owe to people, some of whom I have never even met. But to all whom I have pressurised by letter and by telephone as well as those who have accepted me into their homes, my sincere thanks are due.

I have had wonderful help and cooperation from the Kent Library Service for which I should like to express my gratitude. In particular, I should like to thank the staff at the following libraries: Broadstairs, Canterbury, Chatham, Deal, Dartford, Dover, Faversham, Folkestone, Gravesend, Greenwich, Maidstone, Margate and Tunbridge Wells. The staff of Eastbourne Central Library have as ever shown patience with my requests and once more I am in their debt.

My thanks are also due to the Centre for Kentish Studies; the Centre for Medway Studies; The Guildhall Library, London; The National Maritime Museum; The Whitbread Archives and The Society for Psychical Research.

I am most grateful to Charles Farmer who kindly sent me, a total stranger, some of his collection of cuttings; to Christine Hall who wrote to me about her road ghost; to Don Burgess and David Orchard for all kinds of assistance; to Anne Stapylton and my wife, Anne, for their scrutiny of the draft and their helpful advice.

I must, in particular, acknowledge the help of Kevin and Sandie Carlyon; of the Rev Philip Steff; of Geoff Butler and of Roy Phillips. I have imposed on all of them and each has responded with time and with lengthy documentation. For their patience and their generosity I am truly grateful.

Thanks to each and all.

Foreword

It must be the notion of the unknown and the inexplicable that attracts us to tales of the supernatural, that makes them so completely irresistible. From childhood many of us have felt the thrill, the fear, that come with accounts of phantoms, wraiths, apparitions and all of those occurrences that defy explanation and continue to puzzle us. In our curiosity and entrancement, we are no different from those early men who told their stories in the flickering shadows of caves; no different from balladeers in gaunt castles and old men in village taverns in medieval times. Outside, in those dark years, there were so many impenetrable mysteries and fearsome magics; inside, in the warmth, in the comforting presence of one's fellows, there was the frisson of hearing about what could not be explained. Today, there is still that long tradition of such tales. There is no escaping their pull.

Kent is a county rich in such stories and I have made a selection of those which are of the strongest appeal to me and I hope to readers. So here in addition to some older tales, the reader will find accounts of modern poltergeists; of exorcisms; of spirits of evil at large in a farmhouse and of the phantoms of our roads. Then there is the baffling case of spontaneous human combustion in Folkestone and the equally intriguing experiences of the doctor at Minster in Thanet and the lady in Tunbridge Wells who found themselves transported back in time. And of course there are the ghost ships of the Goodwin Sands; the multiple hauntings of The Pantiles; Humphrey, the ghost of the Theatre Royal at Chatham and 'Sailor Sam' who appears to be so attached to dear old Radio Caroline.

That many of these manifestations are beyond obvious explanation is undeniable and the what and the why of them continue to mystify, as do all of those other curiosities which our rational-minded age finds so exasperating. But, of course, that is why over many years they have never failed to prove other than compelling. I hope that the readers of this book will also find them so.

W. H. Johnson

1

Black Magic at Branden

It was one of those changes of direction that brought Ian Davison to Kent in 1932. For years he had been a successful actor and now he wanted to retire from the stage. He wanted to be out of London, away from the bustle of city life and the insistent demands of the theatre. At heart he knew that he belonged to the country and what he had in mind was a property in some secluded rural retreat where he could farm a little, garden a little, write and entertain his many friends. And one day after he had for months scoured the county for a suitable place, he lit on Branden Farm just outside Sissinghurst.

Yet Branden must have been among the least prepossessing of the properties that he had looked at. There was about it a general air of neglect. The outside of the house was overgrown with nettles and brambles; the weatherboarding and palings were rotten; ivy had loosened many of the tiles of the fine old barn; the oast house was in a similar state of disrepair and the cowsheds had ugly, rusting, corrugated iron roofs. The whole place, with its air of abandonment, was rat-infested. Outside in the garden area lay heaps of tangled iron. Inside, the house was in need of total refurbishment. The building was well over 400 years old and it looked as if in all that time little had been done to keep it in good repair. It was appalling and yet Ian Davison jumped at it. It was just the sort of challenge he felt that he needed at this stage of his life. He would work at it, make it truly his.

Over the next several years Davison was to transform the once-derelict farm into a wonderful home. He had seen the potential beauty of Branden and all the neglect and squalor had not obscured from him what could be done. In the end there was a house, beautiful both inside and out. It was a creation to be proud of. The once overgrown garden now grew primroses and daffodils, primulas and violets, camellias and lupins and Davison's special favourite, irises, blue, gold, purple and bronze. Throughout the year there was always something in the garden to attract the eye.

And the orchard flourished, too, with its apple and cherry trees and its greengages and nuts. 'My land,' said the supremely happy Davison, 'is rich with trees.' And to further please him there were the dogs and cats, the cattle, chickens, pigs and Red Carneaux pigeons.

It was a tremendous achievement to have created so much. And an even greater achievement to have done so when plagued in his first two years in the house by the most malevolent and frightening apparitions.

Right from his arrival at Branden in April 1932 they made their presence known. What is remarkable is the courageous fashion in which the former actor faced up to manifestations that would have driven many another man back to London. Ian Davison's principal response was to take an interest in the whole experience and, even more unusual, to feel some sympathy for two of the ghosts when once he understood their story.

It began on the first night. There was a tapping at the window. Yet when Davison looked out there was no sign of anyone. Certainly it was not a case of a tree branch knocking on the window panes. There was no explanation but Davison, a man who always accepted quite philosophically that there were things in life and nature beyond rational explanation, remained unshaken by the noise. Another evening he heard footsteps outside, then the sound of two men running. Suddenly at the north end of the house was a crash. The chimney was under repair at the time and Davison wondered if it had fallen. Yet when he investigated there was sign neither of damage to any part of the house nor of any intruders. Other nights he heard other sounds: once, a wail of heart-rending agony; another time, a crash as if a heavy piece of furniture had fallen inside the house. In his bedroom at night Davison frequently heard heavy footsteps when he knew there was no one else in the house.

There was something decidedly disconcerting about the place. Davison agreed with his many visitors that there was always the sense that one was being watched, always that uncertain feeling of someone just beyond the corner of the eye, someone waiting. People staying at Branden frequently felt enervated, felt as though their strength was being sapped. Some visitors experienced the most fearful dreams in which they were being strangled. One visitor told Davison that for several days after such a dream she felt completely exhausted.

In fact the whole house had a discordant air about it, something menacing. The smaller of the two downstairs rooms was usually cold even when the fire had been on all day. Yet on some occasions it was unaccountably hot, overpoweringly so. Sometimes in that room Davison and others felt dizzy, on occasion they even fainted. Some experienced extreme tiredness. Something was very obviously wrong but Davison was unable to account for it. The atmosphere of the small room with its changes of temperature, its odd noises, its musty smell, was ultimately so bad that it could be used only as a box room.

But then the larger ground floor room was equally mystifying. One evening, one of Davison's friends dozed off and then woke with a start. He felt that he had been seized by the neck from behind; he felt that someone had tried to strangle him. Other evenings both Davison and another of his friends fainted in the room, which had become suddenly hot and airless. And once, in the dust on the table in this room, there was the imprint of a claw-like hand.

The first ghost appeared to a man and his wife, guests sleeping in Ian Davison's attic bedroom. A woman carrying what appeared to be a tumbler passed through the room. The husband, receiving no reply from the intruder, threw a slipper at her. She promptly disappeared through the wall. Some weeks later at about four o'clock one afternoon, Davison saw the woman for himself in his bedroom. She was wearing grey, a sad-

9

looking creature, simple-looking perhaps. The woman was slightly bent and it seemed as if she was searching for something on the ground. Yet her appearance was so pitiful and unfrightening that Davison, who was remarkably matter of fact as far as apparitions were concerned, felt nothing but an intense pity for her.

After the sad woman's arrival came others, shadows some of them, some vaguely discerned humans, who appeared most often in the large room downstairs although they were seen at random in other parts of the house. One, the most alarming, would come through the wall of the large downstairs room, float across the room and disappear into the fireplace. His entry, usually in mid-evening, was marked by a sudden fall in temperature. He usually stayed in the room for about five minutes. Sometimes his arrival was preceded by a phantom cat which could never be touched.

Davison's first real encounter with this most frightening phantom, however, was in his bedroom. One night he was awakened by a visitor's dog scratching at his bedroom door. He let the animal into the room where it joined Davison's own Great Dane, Peter. Both dogs were clearly disturbed and anxious. Davison, fresh from sleep, then realised that he was sweating profusely in quite unbearable heat. He recalled that when he was awakened by the dog he had been dreaming that the house was on fire. Was it really on fire? Surely it must be for outside it was freezing, snowing, in fact. Such heat could come only from a fire. Then the door to the bedroom became suddenly transparent, appearing to melt away before his eyes, and Davison saw in front of him 'the foulest looking man I have ever set eyes on.'

Davison's visitor, dressed in a curious costume of bright green, brown and red, stood over six feet tall but what arrested the attention was the man's fierce look of hatred and his revolting face with its thick grinning lips and enormous yellow teeth. Pulling himself together Davison yelled: 'Who are you – a fiend of hell?' The apparition replied with a laugh and disappeared as suddenly as he had come. But it was he who so often came into the large room in the evenings.

One of Davison's many friends was Ronald Kaulbeck, explorer and psychic investigator, who was intensely interested in what he was told about the mysterious events at Branden and he agreed to stay there to see if he could cast any light on what was occurring. He was to say later that in the small room he experienced raw fear of a kind he had never known before. Sitting in the room one evening he suddenly started gasping for breath and grasping at his neck. Three others in the room saw around Kaulbeck's neck some faint shadow. A force of some kind was trying to choke him. It took the three others all their strength to release Kaulbeck from whatever it was that was aiming to kill him. Without any doubt the house was not simply occupied by apparitions but by a wholly malevolent demonic power.

Ronald Kaulbeck, unlike some other guests, was undeterred by this terrifying experience. He stayed on at Branden, his curiosity overcoming any sense of self-preservation. In time he and Davison came to recognise the three principal figures among several who haunted the house. First there was the sad little woman; then there was a short, thick-set, ugly little man who Davison somehow felt was also unhappy; and there was the tall horrifying man who was most obviously the source of the evil which permeated Branden Farm.

Over the months Davison, keen to get to the bottom of the house's ills and to know the origins of the apparitions, enlisted the assistance of several mediums and spiritualists. One of them told Davison that Branden housed the spirits of people who had belonged to a black magic coven and who had met there regularly long years ago. She warned him that the spirits were trying to get rid of him in order to possess the house exclusively. If Davison quit Branden now, he was told, it would never again be habitable. If he stayed on in the face of such terrifying manifestations, if he held on to his courage, they and their evil would go in five months. Davison was warned, however, that he was in a highly dangerous situation. If he stayed on he would have to be prepared for the unexpected and when the test came he must not yield to fear.

The alignment of the house, each wall facing a cardinal point of the compass foresquare, was one which appealed to those who indulged in black magic. Furthermore, it was guarded north and west by ponds. The south in particular was protected by a rank smelling ditch, as in black magic rituals the magician faced north. A former ditch had possibly protected the east side of the house. Magic circles guarded the entrances and places where sacrifices, human or animal, were made.

The medium who alerted Davison to the situation also identified his ghosts. The principal apparition, the most terrifying, was George Tarver who must have occupied Branden, perhaps as early as the 16th century. He was a glover who inherited the property from his father, a physician. George Tarver was steeped in black magic, the Grand Master of the coven which met at this house. (It may be recalled that in the 17th century five female witches at nearby Cranbrook were burned and two others from Goudhurst were sentenced to die for keeping 'an evil and wicked spirit in the likeness of a black dog with the intent and purpose that they, by the aid and help of the said evil and wicked spirit, certain evil and devilish arts called Witchcrafts might use against the public peace.') Certainly witchcraft was not unknown in Kent.

Tarver's coven included his mistress, who was driven mad when Tarver used her baby as a human sacrifice. Then tiring of her, he suffocated her and burnt her body in the small downstairs room. Another member of the coven, the small ugly man, now identified as Hunter, disgusted at the turn of events, protested and he too was strangled by the Grand Master and buried in the grounds. The members of the coven who had enjoyed the rituals, the defiance of Christianity, the magic making, the sex orgies, drew the line at what was now happening, They had not become Satanists to commit murder. Something must be done for all of this was getting out of hand. Desperate measures were needed. The coven members took them. They laid hands on their master and they hanged him from a beam in the large room.

Knowing that grisly history can scarcely have reassured

Davison but, nevertheless, he stuck to Branden. By day he went on renovating the house, working the garden, looking after the orchard, developing the small farm. At night he lived with the apparitions.

And then, at last, it all came to an end. It was a late afternoon when the unsuspecting Davison went up to the bathroom for the most momentous of his encounters with Tarver. This day, only a few feet away from the bathroom door, Tarver was waiting, with his menacing smile and on this occasion he looked fearsomely strong. Davison, surprised to see him there, recoiled, afraid of the sheer evil power before him. He wanted to escape, to run down the stairs away from the terrifying figure. Yet just in time he recalled the medium's message. He must be resolute; when the test came he must not yield to his fear. Steeling himself he faced Tarver. 'You must get out of my way! This house is mine! My will is stronger than yours! It does not matter what holds you here! You must leave! Go!' What courage that must have taken.

And Tarver then disappeared, simply faded into the wall. It was his last appearance in human form. The ghost cat, too, which had often preceded or accompanied him, never appeared thereafter.

Three days later the woman appeared in the bathroom and for the first time she looked up at Davison, looked into his face. And she smiled. No longer did she appear sad and downcast. She even looked younger. She stretched out her arms towards him. It was as if she were saying goodbye. He never saw her again.

As for Hunter, he too said a farewell, standing one night by Davison's bed for 20 minutes. But he seemed even sadder than at any other time. At one point he bent over until he almost touched Davison's face. And Davison who had never felt any fear of Hunter, but for whom he had a genuine sympathy, spoke to the apparition, asking if he could help him. At which Hunter without making any kind of response disappeared, never to be seen again.

The ghosts at Branden Farm still for a time manifested themselves in the form of shadows but their appearances became less and less frequent. Finally they ceased to show themselves at all. The house was at peace.

As for Ian Davison, he stayed on at Branden, developing it into a fine house and garden. He had no regrets about choosing it. It was the right place for him in spite of all that had occurred.

2

Stubborn Spirits

The Rev Philip Steff is proud of his work. Small wonder, for he has a significant number of achievements to his name. It is not simply that he is an ordained minister of the Spiritualist Church, nor that he regularly lectures on spiritualism. It is not that he has been featured on TV and radio, nor that newspapers and magazines have shown interest in his work. What seems most important is that Philip Steff is a practical man in such matters, one who accompanies psychic researchers when they investigate hauntings, for it is less easy to deceive someone with the power to 'see' ghosts. Furthermore, he is regularly called upon to release souls stuck in the limbo between this world and the next, as well as to exorcise evil entities from ordinary houses.

Because he is more often successful than not he was glad to be featured in this book. Though when he was told it was about Kent, he laughed. 'Perhaps I should tell you about a couple of failures in that county,' he said. 'It isn't always simple, you know.' That was a refreshing response. And the only proviso was that the true identity of the principals in each case should not be revealed and that they should be referred to by pseudonyms. Remarkably, both Kent ventures took place in June 1999 within a week of each other. This is what Philip told me had happened.

The first case was that of Graham Hammond, a retired civil engineer, who lived in Sittingbourne and who was desperate when he persuaded Philip to help him. He had made several attempts to rid himself of an unwanted spirit in his house. He was of the view that the spirit had come with him from south-east London where he had formerly lived.

On Monday, 7th June 1999, Philip and his assistant of 20 years, Derek Goodson, set out on the excursion from his home in Bath to Sittingbourne. From what Hammond had said it seemed that there was no need for an exorcism. It was more likely in this case that a release was called for. Having already released over 100 souls of people trapped in limbo between this earth and the after life, the two mediums were optimistic of success.

Of course these spirits are not evil, although their presence can be frightening. Sometimes they announce themselves by mysterious footsteps. On other occasions objects are moved from one place to another. Frequently rooms in houses they occupy are cold and no amount of extra heating seems to raise the temperature.

'It's their way of telling you they are there. They are really drawing attention to their plight. You see, spirits do not always reach the Spirit World,' Philip explains, 'and this may be for a variety of reasons. Perhaps they are murdered or they are suicides. It may be that they are too attached to their possessions in this world. Some appear to be men or women who just failed to accomplish something or to complete it before they died.'

It always gives Philip and Derek pleasure to release the earth-bound. 'Although they can see, feel and think,' Philip says, 'there is one thing they fail to appreciate. They do not realise that they are dead. They really need help to leave this place. They don't belong here. They need to understand that they no longer have a physical body. They have a spirit body now. Our task is to persuade them of their situation. I suppose that we're needed to tell them that they are dead – as far as this world is concerned, anyway.'

So this it seemed was what they were to do in Sittingbourne. To persuade a spirit ('George', Graham Hammond had called him) to move on from his earthbound condition.

They arrived at Hammond's two-storey house on the main road just after lunch. Graham Hammond, fit and active for his years, told his visitors almost on arrival that he believed that he had psychic powers. At least that had been suggested to him, but he appeared to have no wish to use them. This information was interesting in view of what transpired.

Philip and Derek were quite convinced that Hammond was being pestered by a spirit which was certainly mischievous but not evil. He played tricks which were infuriating but not malicious. Sometimes in the middle of the night Hammond would be roused by the ringing of the telephone. It was almost as if the instrument were in the bedroom when in fact it was downstairs. At other times there were sounds of scratching under the pillow or even a knocking inside the pillow. The old man was wakened by what at times seemed like electric shocks, the same sort of sensation that is experienced when the funny bone gets a knock.

Hammond said that he had once glimpsed 'George's' head and shoulders. That was the only occasion on which he had seen his tormenter. Philip told me that at this point he interrupted Hammond. 'I quickly asked him not to describe the face as this would colour my mind,' he said. 'You see, good mediums don't like this information in advance.'

'George' apparently had a tendency to interfere with the TV and sometimes the screen would go blank. He seemed particularly biased against BBC2. On at least one occasion Hammond had peremptorily ordered 'George' to put the picture back on and his order was obeyed almost immediately.

After having been given a detailed account of the spirit's behaviour the two mediums next went to every room in the house. They stood silently in each one, absorbing the atmosphere. They were soon persuaded that there was work to be done. Each of them experienced a tingling sensation in the hands and spine in every room they entered.

As it was clear that this was a release and not an exorcism, no further preparations were required. No altar was set up and no protective circle was deemed necessary.

In the presence of Graham Hammond, Philip went into a trance. Derek linked in to him, giving off psychic energy to increase the chances of a successful release. At this point there came into Philip's mind the figure of a bearded man in dark and drab clothing, a man dressed in Victorian fashion. He had about him a disreputable air. He might not have looked out of place as a low-life villain in a Dickens novel.

Now Philip learned the man's story, communicating with him not in words but by the exchange of thoughts. He had hanged himself, the man told Philip. He had committed a crime of which he had felt ashamed. With a partner, he had broken into a house but he had kept the bulk of the money. He had escaped capture but his partner had gone to prison where some years later he had died. The old villain was consumed with guilt.

And now, though he did not know it, he was in that hopeless Nowhere.

Philip's message was to persuade this strange figure that he was now dead and that he could not remain earthbound. Despite some hesitation, the man finally appeared to accept his position and to accept that he ought to move on.

Out of his trance, Philip told Hammond and Derek what had occurred. When he heard the description of the 'villain', Hammond was sure that Philip had met 'George'. Oddly enough, it transpired in the course of their conversation that some years earlier Graham Hammond's wife had hanged herself. There is in Philip's opinion, however, no apparent connection between this sad event and 'George'.

On the way back to Bath both men felt optimistic about the outcome. They were sure that it had been a good day's work. One sign was the state of Derek's hands. At the end of their sessions Philip always asks Derek what his hands feel like. Usually whilst he is working his hands are warm. If, after they have completed a release or an exorcism, Derek's hands cool down fairly quickly they are quite confident of their success. On this occasion Derek's hands were giving off the most encouraging symptoms.

'To my concern and astonishment,' Philip says, 'Mr Hammond phoned a few days later.'

Apparently, 'George' was still playing up. It was baffling and disappointing for Philip as it was his first unsuccessful release. What could have happened? 'George' had given no indication that he would not move on 'into the light'.

Philip's advice to Graham Hammond was simple. It looked as if 'George' was not going to leave so easily. Could it be that he was aware of the psychic powers that Hammond claimed to possess? For if he did have some psychic capacity it might be that 'George' was stirring him up to do something about it. Possibly 'George' was urging Hammond to use his powers, to take up release work. Perhaps he intended to stay with Hammond until he got the point. After all, it would not be the first time that a spirit had 'blackmailed' his victim in this way. Philip urged Hammond to join his local Spiritualist church and to start using his powers.

At the time of writing Philip has not heard from Graham Hammond for several months and so he does not know if his advice has been taken, or for that matter if 'George' is still at it. It was a less satisfactory conclusion than had been hoped for.

The second case involved Walter Banks, a retired accountant, living on his own in Rochester. In a phone call to Philip, Banks said that he was being pestered by a spirit. The disturbances had been going on for a considerable time. In fact he had left his previous home near Canterbury to escape the incessant pressure, the fear which he lived with daily. For some time he had stayed in a guest house and had then come to Rochester. But there was no escape. Whatever was haunting him accompanied him to his new home. Now there were noises in the house, terrible, loud noises which terrified him, noises as loud as thunder. And sometimes there was what seemed like a woman in his bedroom. He could sometimes hear the rustle of her dress.

Some nights, some terrifying nights, as he lay alone in his bed, there was loud whistling; there were unaccountable scratching sounds at the window, and there were more deep-sounding rolls of thunder through the darkened house. And sometimes there was a weight on his chest, pressing down on him so that he could scarcely breathe. Other times he would hear the swish of the dress of the phantom woman and this was always followed by the most enormous, the most deafening crash.

Banks had tried other exorcists, some of them highly recommended, but nothing they did seemed to work. At least, whatever they did had no lasting effect. For a time there would be a period of calm and then the trouble would start all over again. Nothing they did was effective.

Finally Philip Steff agreed to visit Kent from his home in Bath. What Philip knew in advance was that some years earlier Walter Banks had used an ouija board. Whether this had been for fun or for some serious spirit message was not clear. In any case, as far as Philip was concerned, Banks had involved himself in something potentially dangerous. The ouija board is not a toy. It is not a party game. It has the capacity to invite something into the house and that something is not easily got rid of. And it may be something of profound evil. This playing the ouija board, Philip was certain, was the origin of Banks's troubles. Somewhere in the house were entities of ill-intent, what Philip Steff calls 'phantoms of the night', demonic and possibly at times dangerous.

At the same time Philip had the idea from his phone calls with Banks that perhaps the unsuccessful exorcists were not totally responsible for the failure of their ministrations. Perhaps Banks was the kind of man who did not co-operate with those he had called in to help him.

On 14th June 1999, a week after the foray to Sittingbourne, Philip Steff went from Bath to Rochester. This time, and contrary to practice, he was unaccompanied. Neither Derek nor anyone else could fit in the trip to Rochester with him.

As he entered Walter Banks's small, neat bungalow Philip at once experienced a strong tingling in both of his hands. From long experience he knew what that signified. There was certainly something there. And he sensed that it was decidedly nasty.

Philip set up a small altar on the bedroom table on which he also placed candles, a crucifix and a model shrine made of cardboard and with the appearance of a church. There was even a stained glass window illuminated by a candle standing behind. Next he took out of his bag a large ring of calico on which were written in large letters the names of the four archangels – Uriel, Michael, Rafael, Gabriel. Walter Banks was seated in a chair inside the ring. After prayer and a reading from Ephesians 6, Philip called upon the four archangels to help him with the task of cleansing the house of its evil spirits. His Spirit Guide, his 'doorkeeper' Serenghi, was as always present.

But at the end of it all, it had not gone well. Philip was aware of that. Before he left Rochester he had considerable doubts about the effectiveness of his afternoon's work. No doubt he was exhausted, his own psychic batteries in need of recharging and he was less than pleased with Banks, who during the long and draining exorcism had contrived to fall asleep! Had the entities themselves made him doze off, he wondered? And had the entities, as they sometimes do, hidden during the exorcism? Had they done so, they would have escaped.

Two days later a disgruntled Banks rang to say that nothing had changed. And why, he wanted to know, had Philip bothered with all that religious rigmarole? That was no use, Banks said. Well, Philip told him, he ought to be patient. Sometimes after an exorcism the evil spirits have a brief period of retaliation before they go. Walter Banks was less than impressed with that answer.

Some weeks later, however, Banks rang Philip once again. The thunder had stopped, he said, and he was keeping the entities away by leaving on his TV at night for they are known not to like the light.

And Philip Steff was able to smile wryly. Not a total success, he thought, but perhaps not a complete failure.

3

The Grey Lady of Cleve Court

How frequently ghosts have their origin in stress and unhappiness. People thrown out of work, jilted lovers, victims of the cruellest deceptions – small wonder that they carry their wretchednesses with them, across lawns and landings, in bedrooms and cellars. We can think of Old Thorndyke who hanged himself when his firm, Mackesons, left Hythe and who now haunts the Malthouse Arcade; then, there is poor Mlle Pinard, rejected by her soldier lover during the Napoleonic Wars and who now, dressed in orange silk, walks Steel Lane in Meopham; another is the dairymaid, pregnant by a priest, who committed suicide at Old Soar Manor. There are so many whose deep pain is seemingly endless. The Grey Lady of Cleve Court carries her burden of sadness, too.

The house, located in a secluded part of Minster in Thanet, was purchased in 1920 by Sir Edward Carson, the celebrated lawyer and politician. In recent years, as a member of the government, he had been deeply involved in the Ulster 'troubles'. Now a quieter life beckoned and the house on King William's Mount with its stunning views was the ideal spot.

Cleve Court was an interesting house, part of it early Tudor, part Elizabethan and part 18th century. The Carsons very much liked it. Whilst there were occasional unaccounted-for occurrences – footsteps at night like those of a woman in high heels; tapping at night at their bedroom door when the house was occupied solely by the Carsons – they had no reservations about living there. In fact, Lord Carson (he had been ennobled shortly after settling at Cleve Court) had a rational explanation for the footsteps and tappings: when houses stretched at night there were always odd noises. When a guest heard what seemed like drawers opening and shutting above her bedroom even though she was on the top floor, Lord Carson was able to satisfy himself with an explanation. It was Lady Carson who was convinced of the supernatural origin of these sounds. Even so, she was not alarmed for the house was in no way sinister. It never gave off the disconcerting vibrations felt, for example, at Branden.

Remarkably, it was children who were first aware of the Grey Lady. Edward, the Carsons' son, slept in the Elizabethan wing of the building. When he was five years old and had been sleeping in the same bedroom for four years, he told his mother one day that he did not like the lady who walked at nights in the passage outside his bedroom door. What was she like, his mother wanted to know, but the boy was unable to say. She always walked away, he said.

At the age of four, Edward's cousin, Patricia Miller, came to stay and she slept in the Elizabethan bedroom. She told Lady Carson of the lady who came to stand by the bed. And if only her aunt would look in the corner at that very moment – There! Now! In the corner! the child insisted – she would see that the lady was standing there. When her aunt told Patricia that she could not see anything the child was extremely angry. Why did she not see the lady? She was all too plainly there, the little girl said. Suffice it to say that this nursery bedroom became known as 'the ghost room'. Dogs showed a marked reluctance to enter it, and the feeling soon spread amongst the servants.

Another member of the family, the six or seven year old Diana Colvin, when asked back to Cleve Court asked her aunt if 'the poor lady' would be there. The poor lady who walked in and out of the room, Diana explained, the one to whom no one spoke. 'No one tells me who she is,' she complained, adding that she had also seen her walking in and out of the drawing room during the day.

In 1949, an adult in the house had a curious experience. The wife of the young Edward Carson had taken a bath when all others in the household were in bed. She had just left the bathroom when she heard someone coming along the passage towards her. The footsteps came nearer and nearer, right up to her, and then they passed her, receding down the passageway. But no one was to be seen.

Later in the year, in the very early hours of the morning, Lady Carson's spaniel, Susan, woke her mistress. The dog wanted to go out. Lady Carson got out of bed and prepared to let the spaniel out in the grounds. As she went downstairs in this, the Georgian part of the house, she inadvertently brushed against the light switch and put out the light. For some unexplained reason Lady Carson did not bother to put it on again. At the foot of the stairs the dog decided that it would go no further and to discover what was wrong Lady Carson now switched on the light. The dog was obviously afraid of something. Lady Carson then looked back up the staircase and saw the figure coming down.

It was a woman. She was wearing a very full grey skirt down to her feet. Round her neck and shoulders she wore a very pale grey cape. In her hair was a piece of white ribbon. Even though the woman averted her face, Lady Carson could see that she was young. She looked very solid; she was 'quite material in every way'. The figure now turned on the landing and went into the Elizabethan part of the house. But there was a coldness in the air and the experience terrified Lady Carson.

In December 1949 these two incidents received wide coverage in the newspapers. They also produced an interesting response. EC – she did not give her full name – wrote to *The Times* to say that at the age of 15 she was working at Cleve Court. It was her first job and she was under-housemaid. One day she had been asked to prepare a room at the end of the passage as a nursery for a visiting child. It was early in the morning, about seven o'clock, when she was in the room and she heard footsteps outside the door. EC looked up to see a lady in an old-fashioned dress peering in at her. Thinking it was one of the guests the girl made as if to leave. But no, the lady waved one hand as if to tell her simply to carry on with her work and went on. When EC mentioned this to another of the maids later in the day her remarks were pooh-poohed. She had been mistaken. There was no one in the house wearing a long, old-fashioned dress. And the young housemaid accepted what her older colleague had told her. Only now, after 45 years, and after reading about the recent events at Cleve Court, did EC realise who it was that she had seen. And she also now understood the reason for the brusque response she had received from the other maid who clearly had not wished to frighten her.

Despite the fact that Lady Carson had received a terrible fright she would have no truck with the idea that the house should be rid of its ghost. 'You see,' she said, 'we like our ghost. She does no harm.' After all, children had told her for years about the Grey Lady and none of them had come to harm. The atmosphere of the house was in no way affected by the presence of the ghost. Even the family physician, Dr Moon, who had a most odd experience at Cleve Court (described elsewhere in this book) nevertheless agreed that the atmosphere was always pleasant.

Lady Carson never again saw or heard the ghost of Cleve Court. But in 1966, Andrew Mackenzie, researching the story, received a letter from Mr and Mrs Rigden, gardener and maid at the house. 'About the footsteps at Cleve Court, yes, they are still heard, and very plain at times,' the Rigdens wrote. ' You hear them come to the bedrooms in the old part of the house, mostly after midnight ... These footsteps were heard last week by a woman now living in the old part and she told us both she had heard footsteps.'

The most likely candidate for the role of the Grey Lady of Cleve Court is the much put-upon wife of Josias Fuller Farrer who in 1762, when still a minor, inherited the house and a fortune of £100,000 from his father. This premature inheritance was his downfall although it must be admitted that it was long years before he ran through it. The young man is said to have 'converted it (the house) into a scene of riot and extravagance almost incredible'. Cleve was an open house 'where all kinds of visitors who could amuse or be amused were welcome.' There were seldom fewer than 40 guests with their servants. For himself Farrer 'maintained 30 horses in his stables for various purposes: drove six in his carriage, with out-riders mounted and furnished with french horns; kept hounds and hunters, and even a seraglio of women for the accommodation of his visitors. When his cellars overflowed with wine, butts were deposited to ripen in the out-offices, and when required for use, too frequently found emptied by the train of rascal attendants.' Each fortnight three butts of ale were delivered to Cleve and very often even this was insufficient for Farrer and the countless hangers-on who drank and ate their way through the fortune. Some local tradesmen are said to have dated their prosperity from the days of Josias Fuller Farrer, who in time found himself reduced to comparative want.

But his wife and his only son? Where were they at this time of riotous extravagance? Certainly they did not share in the merrymaking. What wife could, knowing the kinds of women that her husband invited to the house? According to some accounts, whilst scenes of depravity and licence were enacted below, she was exiled upstairs and locked in her room.

Reports of the Cleve Court ghost, that sad and lonely woman, have her looking fondly at the children in the nursery bedroom. Perhaps isolated in her own room, ignored and scorned by a brutally selfish husband, she had sought comfort from the only possible source, her own sleeping child. Her deep distress at her situation echoed down the years. In the Carsons and their children she did at least find people who had some sympathetic feeling for her. Nevertheless, there is a matter to be considered. If ghosts have feelings carried over from their lifetimes – and this particular story hints that they do – perhaps Cleve's Grey Lady ought to have been laid to rest. Perhaps it is not enough to say that 'we like our ghost' and leave her to trail a sad way down endless years.

4

Spontaneous Human Combustion in Folkestone

Reg Gower pushed the door tentatively and went into the room, sniffing for smoke. After all, he was the landlord and his tenant might have left something burning on the oven top. Best to be sure. He might even be asleep though that was unlikely at 10.30 in the morning. But now he was inside there was a powerful smell of smoke, and perhaps it was then or perhaps a little later that Mr Gower noticed the thin layer of greasy moisture on the windows and the flat surfaces of the room. The polystyrene kitchen tiles were slightly charred as was a small plastic air vent. But there was little sign of serious fire damage. On the gas ring, still lit, a kettle, half full, was boiling. There was little else of note if one discounted the polythene brush and dustpan, both totally undamaged, which were no more than a few inches away from the pile of ashes that was once the body of Barry Soudaine. All else that remained of Mr Gower's tenant was one foot and a trainer.

Only two days after Christmas 1987, it was a particularly bad time, an extraordinarily sad time, for such a lonely, ugly death. Barry Soudaine, a bachelor who worked in the bakery below his flat in Canterbury Road as a cleaner and general handyman, was only 44 years of age after all and his end was horrific. His body had been consumed in fire of elemental ferocity, yet it had been so localised that the room in which he was found was scarcely touched.

The police not unnaturally considered the possibility of

murder. Had Soudaine been done to death elsewhere, they wondered, his body burned, and then transferred to his flat at the baker's shop in the centre of Folkestone? But that was preposterous for the body was so profoundly burnt that it could not have been lifted. It would have disintegrated completely, so that even its present vague human shape could not have been maintained. In that event the police had to determine whether someone had broken into the flat and murdered the victim. But there was no sign of any break-in. Murder as a possibility was out. And so was suicide for there was no evidence anywhere in the flat of petrol or any other fire accelerant.

Clearly, the police decided, the dead man had had a heart attack and as he fell, he had stumbled against the lit gas stove. He had caught fire with obviously disastrous consequences. He had burnt to death, his body consumed over the space of perhaps 15 hours. He had been seen the previous evening at about 7.30. It must have been shortly after that time that he had his tragic fall. At least this was the police view. Unsurprisingly, from the outset they had rejected the notion of spontaneous human combustion (SHC). Just as, over the years, many fire officers and medical men and coroners have turned their backs on such an absurd suggestion.

Yet the Home Office pathologist, Dr Heath, did not dismiss the possibility of SHC out of hand, saying at the post mortem that further investigations were necessary. And at the Coroner's Court a verdict of accidental death was rejected. The destruction of the rest of the body was so complete that it was impossible to say how the man had died. There was no medical history of heart disease and along with the remainder of the organs, with the exception of the lungs, the heart had been destroyed. An open verdict, rare in these circumstances, was recorded.

Jenny Randles and Peter Hough are serious professional researchers into matters which might be described as the supernatural and the paranormal. They bring to their work a tireless doggedness and a critical scientific approach. They are not out to support crackbrained flimflam but at the same time they do not dismiss out of hand what many may describe as cranky notions. The objectivity of scientific method has been a feature of their work over several years. When Barry Soudaine died in December 1987 they had already been investigating SHC for five years. Although there had been many claims for it, the evidence somehow was never totally convincing. How could it be accepted, this curious notion that people, without warning and without any interference, suddenly burst into flames. But if absolute proof had been hard to come by, the Soudaine case at last seemed to present compelling evidence that the phenomenon, which for well over a hundred years had been the subject of spasmodic debate in some quarters, ought to be taken seriously.

After the inquest the two researchers asked to see the police photographs of the scene at the Folkestone flat but their request was refused. They were told that the pictures were 'pornographic' with their hideous detail of the incinerated corpse. They did, however, have more success with the Coroner who presided at the inquest. He said that he could not rule out SHC as the cause of Soudaine's death. It was a possibility but of course the more or less total destruction of the body could not permit him to reach such a verdict.

But Randles and Hough have brought the Soudaine case positively into the debating chamber for there were a number of factors which needed to be considered. Take the kettle on the gas ring when Mr Gower entered the room and which was still there when the police arrived. Who half filled the kettle? Who lit the gas? Who at some point shifted the kettle so that only half of it was on the ring? The answer is Barry Soudaine and that has never been in dispute.

So when did he put it there? The matter of timing is crucial. The police were of the view that it must have taken at least 15 hours to reduce the body to the state in which they found it. Hence the kettle must have been placed on the stove at least 15 hours before it was found. But how long would it take a kettle on a gas ring to run dry? How long would it take to burn through the bottom? Can there be any doubt that if the kettle had been on the ring for 15 hours it would have boiled dry and the bottom would have been holed? Randles and Hough believe that the kettle must have been placed on the gas ring no more than an hour or two before. What they say in effect is that the body of Barry Soudaine was reduced to ashes in a very short space of time.

The condition of the body must next be considered. Jenny Randles and Peter Hough consulted a crematorium superintendent who found it difficult to accept that a mere house fire could have wreaked such havoc on a body. She had seen a BBC programme which attempted to debunk the idea of SHC but which did include photographs of the remains of some victims. They were so reduced; there was in effect nothing left, no skeletal remains. There was for the most part nothing but ash. The superintendent told the two researchers how corpses are cremated in heat of up to nearly 1,000 degrees for one and a half hours. But some bones always remain. Pelvis and thigh bones, ball and socket joints, are not converted into ash. They subsequently have to be ground down after the cremation process is complete.

The question was: could such a fire, of such intensity occur in a house? Most house fires leave something recognisable. Even in the worst kinds of motor accidents when the engine explodes and it is impossible to rescue the occupants there are remains of bones and sometimes flesh. What kind of fire was this that could so degrade a body, so eat it up, and yet not seriously damage the surroundings? Mrs Valerie Bennett, that experienced superintendent to whom the researchers had addressed themselves, was to say: 'I cannot see how a human body could generate sufficient heat to turn a room into a cremator.' And an expert fire officer expressed the opinion that the 'amount of heat required to degrade these bones would be so intense that surrounding areas should ignite'.

So here is a mystery. Did Barry Soudaine really meet his death by SHC, just by bursting into flames, without warning, without any external source to ignite him? But what is it that causes such an outrageous phenomenon? The trouble is that while cases appear to go back to the 17th century there is so little hard evidence. Often there are no witnesses and there have been few survivors. What few witnesses there are attest to a bluish flame coming from the abdominal area. The fire begins inside the body and works its way out. It goes on to consume the body, to reduce it to the finest ash, and yet the fire does not spread to the surroundings. Some body fat, moisturised, is found on window glass and on flat surfaces but otherwise the effects of the burning are not seen much beyond the body.

But what is the cause of this internal fire, this fierce raging inferno inside the abdomen? Is it something quite beyond the normal and the natural? One witness, a doctor, said of the visible effects of SHC: 'Were I living in the Middle Ages, I'd mutter something about black magic'. For how can our innards cause such an eruption?

Is it something supernatural, something paranormal? One example from beyond Kent may suggest that it is. In January 1899 two sisters, Alice, 5 years old, and Amy Kirby, 4, were living in different houses at Sowerby Bridge near Halifax. Because their parents had separated, Alice went to live with her father and grandmother while Amy stayed with her mother in a house a mile away. At 11 o'clock on 5th January Amy's mother went out of the house to get water from the nearby well. She was away from the house for no more than two minutes. When she returned she found Amy screaming, engulfed in flames. At the identical moment, one mile away, Alice was found with flames three feet high coming out of her head. It is difficult to seek and accept some rational and scientific answer in view of what happened to these little girls. At the inquest the Coroner used words like 'strange', 'remarkable', and 'shocking coincidence' but made no reference to SHC. In the same way, the police dismissed any suggestion of it in the case of Barry Soudaine.

There are many other examples of SHC though perhaps none exemplifies the possibility of paranormal causes in quite the way the case of the Kirby girls does. And Barry Soudaine's death does seem to indicate the speedy ferocity of such a fire that reduces its victims to ash and cinder. Some have suggested poltergeist activity for this is often associated with outbreaks of fire but that, however, would be to deny the internal origin of the flames.

The classic features of SHC, those elements noticed in so many instances, were present when Barry Soudaine died. There was intense heat, little damage to the near surroundings and the massive destruction of the body. Some will produce theories about combustible gases in the digestive system; others will claim surges of excess electrical energy in the body. But some will claim more sinister though inexplicable causes. In the paranormal, in the supernatural, will lie the cause for these people.

5

Danger on the Roads

Some years ago an old local, asked about Lord Rokeby, the headless horseman, whose four panting horses breathe fire as they race along Stone Street near Postling crossroads, was quite frank. 'No, I can't say I ever seed 'im – and dunnosiwanto,' he said. 'Reckon I'd run away. I knewed a man what did see 'im an' it gran' nigh druv 'im off 'n 'is 'ead!' Not surprising, perhaps.

And there is more than Lord Rokeby on the roads of Kent. There have been constant reports of ghostly activity on the county's highways and byways. There are phantom coaches and headless horsemen at Rainham, Pluckley, Grafty Green, Sissinghurst, Oxney, Eastwell Park and other places, too.

Yet nowadays the phantom coachmen and the ghostly highwaymen of the past are almost a kind of quaintly acceptable fancy dress parade. Most of them have not been seen for years. The fact is that we are more disconcerted by modern-day apparitions and other inexplicable supernatural happenings along our highways. They are less easy to laugh off, more difficult to explain away so glibly. The roads of today carry so many mysteries associated with the recent past. Where once there were coaches and highwaymen we now have motor cars and motor car victims. It is in our encounters with these that we have to confront our beliefs and doubts.

There are so many curious occurrences involving cars. What about the driver who at Bewl Bridge in 1997 saw the headlights of a car coming down the hill in her direction? She slowed down to give the oncoming vehicle room to pass. But there was nothing save the sound of the engine which passed her. And when it did so, her audio cassette jumped out of the player. Of course, there might have been a rational explanation. The approaching car might have turned off before reaching her. But the driver swore she heard the car engine as it passed by and equally mysteriously there was the odd mechanical response. And odd mechanical responses are not rare. On the difficult bend on Elchin Hill at Elmstead, brakes have failed and steering has refused to respond on several occasions. This is not the only location for such an unusual experience.

What causes engine, steering or brake failure? The answer in many instances is bad maintenance or poor driving. Yet this cannot totally account for the curious loss of power experienced by some motorists at particular spots over the years. Take that stretch of road near the crossing of the A253 from Ramsgate to Canterbury and the A256 going south from Margate. At this point there have been several serious motor accidents. In 1922 an accident here in which two women drivers were killed made front page news. At the inquest witnesses said that despite good visibility both cars seemed unable to stop. Examination of the cars revealed no mechanical faults and nothing to explain what had occurred.

On another occasion, in 1936, at these same crossroads a constable on point duty signalled an approaching motor cyclist to slow down as he came to the junction. But the motor cycle continued without reducing speed. Just before he collided with the policeman the cyclist was heard to call out that he could not stop. Fortunately neither the policeman nor the motor cyclist was badly hurt. There was nothing to explain the cyclist's inability to control his machine, nothing to say why he had been unable to brake or steer away from the constable.

The above are two of several such accidents at this road junction. That there should be accidents is hardly surprising: it is their nature which is so remarkable. It is astonishing to discover that most of the cars involved in such incidents have been found on inspection to be properly maintained and to have no readily identifiable mechanical fault.

Some students of the paranormal have attributed the numerous accidents on this part of the road to long past events. At times a glowing light has been seen going along this road, crossing by the junction and then transforming itself into a robed shape, but there is no explanation of whom this may be. It may well have some bearing on the unaccountable events at this crossroads. Do the accidents here have anything to do with the fact that at one time a gibbet stood where the roundabout is now? Corpses of hanged criminals were exposed there for weeks, sometimes for months and, it is said, criminals and suicides were once buried at this spot. Such pressures from the past, such depths of sadness and terror, may, it is thought, exert an influence on the present. Can such ancient horror be seared into the very atmosphere?

*   *   *   *

There can be no more terrible experience for the car driver than to come suddenly upon a pedestrian in his path and instinctively know that he will be unable to stop in time. One late night in 1976 a woman driver was driving through Ide Hill, near Brasted. All at once, as she was passing the entry to Chains Farm, she saw a man in motor cycle leathers standing in the road only yards in front of her. She knew that she had no chance of avoiding the motor cyclist. Desperately she slammed on her brakes but it was too late. She drove straight into him. She drew to a halt and got out of the car. But there was nothing to see. No young man, no scattered possessions. And her car bore no signs of damage.

When she reported the matter to the police at Sevenoaks they showed no signs of doubt or disbelief. They were quite accustomed to 'accidents' of that nature on that stretch of road, they said. But they did tell her that a young motor cyclist had a year or two earlier been the victim of a hit and run driver.

On 14th June 1979 an elderly pedestrian was knocked down in Maidstone Road, Sevenoaks. A witness to the 'accident' swore that the driver had no warning and that he could not have avoided the old lady. Save that no body was found nor were there any indications of damage on the bodywork of the car. On the same date, 20 years earlier, there had been an accident at the same spot. An old lady had been killed.

Christine Hall, a writer and lecturer living in Sandhurst, had a slightly different experience late one February night in 1997. She had been to a Women's Institute meeting in the Maidstone area giving a talk and demonstration of belly-dancing and was driving home via Headcorn and Tenterden. As it had begun to drizzle she was driving slowly, taking extreme care, and it was near St Michael's that she was suddenly alerted to a pedestrian. Christine takes up the account of what occurred: 'I could see the man walking on the left side of the road very clearly. He was walking towards me, at first along the road, then into the road. I thought "He's drunk" and I swerved so that I did not hit him.

'When I got close, I could see right through him. He was still there, not only his outline, but his clothes, his face, but they were all see-through. This must have been a very brief moment, during which he was first in front of the car and then on my left, but it seemed long. I was relieved to have avoided an accident and full of amazement at being able to see through him. Then he was gone, just disappeared.

'There's no reason why I should have imagined it – I wasn't thinking about ghosts or about accidents at the time. If my imagination had played a trick on me, I'm sure it would have been the usual story of actually hitting the man in an accident, and it would surely have been a more exciting ghost, say a Celtic warrior or a Roman centurion in full armour. But this one was just a 20th century man – slim, in black, tight clothes which reminded me of the style young men wore in the Fifties. It wasn't a spectacular looking ghost at all.'

Not then an accident – can Christine Hall have swerved and missed her phantom pedestrian? There appears to be no record of an earlier fatal accident at this spot although Andrew Green who has written extensively about Kent's ghosts has said that he has heard of a number of witnesses who had a similar experience in this locality.

Perhaps Oxney's Grey Lady does not quite fit into this category for she is without doubt of the pre-motor car age. Nevertheless, in the course of her wanderings from the woods at Oxney Bottom and towards Eastry, she crosses the Dover road and she has been driven through by at least one car driver, a bus driver and a motor cyclist.

* * * *

However, the most well known of Kent's accident 'victims' appears at Blue Bell Hill. It is said that the figure which appears with startling suddenness in front of drivers is the ghost of a young woman killed in a road accident in November 1965. Four girl friends had spent the afternoon trying on dresses for a forthcoming wedding. In the evening they went out to a pub to meet the bride's fiance. They had been on their way for only a very short time when their Cortina skidded on a treacherous bend near the pedestrian bridge over Old Chatham Road on the A229 north of Maidstone. They collided with another car and three of the girls were killed.

Since this appalling accident there have been many sightings of a girl in the road. Worse still, there have been several phantom accidents. One night in 1974 a highly agitated Maurice Goodenough of Rochester reported to his local police station. He had just run down a young girl on Blue Bell Hill, he said. Only yards away from where the four young women had had their terrible accident nine years earlier, he had driven into a child with 'sickening force'. She was no more than ten years old, he thought, wearing a white blouse, skirt and white ankle socks. He had been unable to get help from passing motorists who ignored his desperate attempts to flag them down and, afraid to move her but reassured that her injuries were less serious than he had feared, Goodenough had bundled up the girl in a tartan rug and left her at the roadside while he drove to the police to seek help. The girl had jumped out so suddenly, he told the police, that he had no chance to stop in time.

Yet when the police accompanied Goodenough to the scene

of the accident there was nothing there but a blanket. But she could not have walked away, the driver insisted. He had gone into her with some force. It was inconceivable that she should simply get up and walk off. And anyway, walk off where? She must have been in need of hospital attention for her forehead and knees were bleeding and the child was obviously shaken. Had someone picked her up? But why was Maurice Goodenough's car undamaged? Was he mistaken? And who was she? She was too young to be the ghost of one of the young women killed on that stretch of road in 1965. And he had carried her to the road side, actually lifted her from the ground. But if it had been a real accident, why was there no subsequent report from a hospital or from the girl's parents?

Among the more recent phantom accidents is the experience of Ian Sharpe. On 10th November 1992, late at night, he was driving near the Aylesford turn-off on the Maidstone-bound carriageway on Blue Bell Hill. Without warning he saw a young girl appear in the road in front of him. She ran towards him. There was nothing he could do. It was all so sudden. Just before she disappeared under the bonnet of the car she seemed to stare straight at him, looking him straight in the eye. After skidding to a halt, Sharpe looked under the car for she must surely be there. But there was no sign of anyone. Frantically he searched the bushes at the side of the road but again there was no evidence of anyone injured. Desperate, just as Maurice Goodenough had been all those years earlier, he attempted to flag down cars but none of them would stop.

Ian Sharpe, understandably worried and shaken, reported the matter to the police. Together they went back to the place where Sharpe told them he had had his accident. They made a search of the area but found no sign of any injured girl. Nor were there any marks on the car. The police, apparently not too surprised at what had occurred, explained that such incidents were not unknown on this stretch of road. But, Sharpe said, she was 'not like a ghost'. She looked solid, human. One thing was certain, he said: 'It was the most scary experience of my life.'

Only two weeks later, on 24th November, at 11 o'clock at night,

19 year old Chris Dawkins had a similar experience. He had driven through Blue Bell Hill village on his way to Maidstone and was passing the Robin Hood Lane junction when a woman wearing a red scarf ran out into his path. She vanished in front of his car, seeming to fall underneath it. After the collision he stopped near the Lower Bell pub and went back to look for the accident victim. Finding no sign of any accident he telephoned his father and the police. There was a thorough search of the area but no dead or injured pedestrian could be found.

Still, Chris Dawkins was as convinced as other motorists had been that he had run over a woman. 'She ran in front of the car,' he said. 'She stopped and looked at me. There was no expression on her face. Then I hit her and it was as if the ground moved apart and she went under the car. I thought I had killed her because it wasn't as if she was see-through. She was solid – as real as you are.' And quite the same thing happened to Paula Cooper who was motoring up the hill early one Sunday morning in June of the following year. A figure ran out in front of her and she too thought she had hit someone. Again, a search of the area by the police produced nothing and as ever the car had not been damaged. How similar this is to other reports.

Over the last 30 years many incidents on Blue Bell Hill have been reported and the police now accept and their reports conclude that motorists have encountered a ghost. In fact more than one ghost has been met in the area of Blue Bell Hill. In 1969 David Smith of Rochester told the *Evening Post* of how on three or four occasions when driving on Blue Bell Hill he had seen two pedestrians walking up the hill. Although they looked solid enough they had simply vanished when he was within four or five yards. 'Once I saw them walking down the hill on the side opposite the pavement,' he said. 'I was driving down the hill at the time and suddenly saw them walk straight across the road in front of an oncoming vehicle. The car drove straight through them and no trace of them was left.' Unlikely? Not on Blue Bell Hill it seems.

On a foggy night in January 1993 a couple in a car saw a haggard old woman, wearing clothing described as old-fashioned, walk into the Chatham-bound carriageway. The figure stopped in the middle of the road with her back to them. Then, as the driver slowed down the old woman turned round. Angela Maiden, a passenger in the car driven by her husband, spoke of an 'overwhelming sense of evil and horror'. The Maidens described the apparition's small, wizened face. The eyes were close-set, small, round and black. 'Then,' their description went on, 'it began to sneer. It had an enormous mouth which was totally black and then it hissed and lifted its arm and began shaking twigs at us as if it was putting a curse on us. The hissing was really loud and seemed to fill the car.' As fast as he was able Mr Maiden pulled away and at the same time the figure seemed to disappear.

A police search found nothing although they admitted that they had two or three similar calls that evening. Was it a hoax? Was some prankster loose that night? Do pranksters dress up and cross into the middle of excessively busy roads on foggy nights in January? Perhaps they do. But then, a taxi driver, Colin Eacott, had days earlier seen a similar figure and, later, the Renolds family had an encounter with the old woman. Mrs Denise Renolds had initially thought that the figure she saw on the roadside, waving what appeared to be heather, was a man dressed up. Certainly, she was sure that this was no gypsy. Her brother-in-law drove up the hill ten minutes later but there was no sign of any old woman at the roadside.

The phenomenon of the phantom hitchhiker is experienced throughout the world, so perhaps unsurprisingly for the past 30 years a young woman at the top of Blue Bell Hill has thumbed a lift to Maidstone. She sits in the rear seat of the car and when the driver pulls up to let her out at her destination she is not there. Despite the number of instances reported there are inevitable doubts about the hitchhiker. How is it that she always seems to occupy a back seat? If she were in the front the driver would see her getting out. Is there no sustained conversation which, when it suddenly ends, might attract the attention of the driver before reaching the destination? Why is it that the hitchhiker always attracts single drivers? Nevertheless, there have been so many reports of the phantom hitchhiker on Blue Bell Hill that the possibility of her existence is difficult to dismiss outright.

On the notorious Oxney Bottom stretch of road between Dover and Deal and known as the Haunted Highway, the Grey Lady has been frequently seen by drivers who have slowed down for her. Some years ago she was described by Martin Husk as 'an old lady dressed in a dark grey cloak hobbling on the nearside of the road.' As he passed her, 'she appeared to go into the thick undergrowth alongside the verge'. But at Christmas 1958 Tom Relf, the conductor on a double decker bus bound for Deal, had an experience that quite unnerved him. 'I was inside the lower deck,' he said. 'When the bus stopped at Oxney Bottom someone boarded the vehicle and went upstairs.' But when he went to collect the fare from the new passenger, the upper deck was empty. His driver later confirmed that they had stopped at Oxney Bottom and that they had taken on a passenger in dark clothes. Had the Grey Lady become another phantom hitchhiker?

Phantom hitchhikers and phantom victims, vehicles that unaccountably malfunction: all related to terrifying accidents, to head-on crashes and mangled pedestrians. The violence of such horrific events, the last-second agonies of those involved, seem to have impressed themselves so deeply on the very places where they occur that down the years they are somehow required to play themselves over and over again, time after time after time.

6

Investigations by a White Witch

The staff at the new Post Office Counters Distribution Centre, built at Aylesford in 1994, seemed from the very earliest days to have more than an unfair share of ill-luck. In fact, in many cases, it was too slight a term to call it ill-luck; it was very serious personal misfortune which in some instances was deeply damaging to those involved. In the first three years of the building's existence each one of the 23 employees experienced alarming personal disturbances. There was a variety of tragic domestic and work-related problems. There were illnesses, break-downs, marital problems, the unexpected deaths of relatives, broken hearts and a whole range of other dramatically upsetting matters. There seemed to be no accounting for such adversity. No one had ever before experienced such a run of troubles, spread as it was right across the workforce. It was certainly beyond any reasonable expectation, far beyond coincidence. And not unnaturally the men and women working there began to talk among themselves, speculating about what might be the cause of so many unhappy afflictions. As one of them said at the time: 'You try every rational explanation but it's been three years now and everyone in regular contact with this place suffers from it.'

What the employees had begun to feel was that there was something extraordinary about their workplace. It was new, a modern industrial unit which ought to have been a pleasure to work in, but it was somehow depressing. There were even some who believed that they had seen apparitions in the building. It was almost, some staff dared to think, as if it was cursed. There were suggestions that these worries ought to be addressed to senior officials but there was some fear about how such concerns might be received. What were people at head office going to think if they received a letter from staff at Aylesford saying that they thought the building was cursed? It was likely to be dismissed as silly, hysterical nonsense.

And it was at that point, in the summer of 1997, that someone proposed calling in Kevin Carlyon. Some of them had read about him in the newspapers; others had seen him at times on Meridian News or heard him on the radio. Why not ask him if he could help? It would be unofficial, of course. No one at head office would be likely to sanction calling in a witch. But it was worth a try and so they contacted him at his home in St Leonards.

Kevin Carlyon would prefer, by the way, not to be described as a 'white witch'. 'Practitioner of Earth Magic' is what he calls himself, though he accepts the other title as a better understood and perhaps more convenient shorthand. He is High Priest of The Covenant of Earth Magic, the world's largest coven. He believes in the power of the earth's energy and it is this which he invokes as he practises healing ills both physical and psychic and as he intercedes on behalf of those experiencing a wide range of other difficulties.

But in imagining him, forget the witches you have read about. Put out of your mind the sinister figures of plays and films. Kevin Carlyon is a very large, amiable sort of man with a blonde pony-tail. According to one of his friends, he looks more like the lead guitarist of Iron Maiden than a witch. Others see some resemblance in this 6 feet 4 inch man to an American wrestler. But Kevin is realistic and practical, a man who is cautious about responding to every call to get rid of troublesome ghosts or evil spirits. He says that sometimes pubs have called him in simply to confirm a non-existent ghost. Ghosts apparently can be good for business. But when he received the call for help from the staff at Aylesford he was convinced that there was something genuinely troubling them.

On 17th July 1997, accompanied by his wife Sandie, the priestess of the coven, and Doug Kempster of the *Sunday Mirror*, Kevin went to the building at Aylesford. There they were met by two of the managers who took them inside in the early evening after all staff had gone home.

The two witches began by visiting every room, sprinkling water around the edges, and in each one leaving crystals charged at nearby Kit's Coty, a neolithic burial ground. This was to ensure the building's protection from alien and evil influences. It was in the kitchen that they had the most curious sensation, for here the temperature had fallen dramatically. It was, says Kevin, 'like a freezer'. And it was in this room that the hair on the back of Sandie's and Doug Kempster's heads stood up on end as though they had suddenly received an electric shock. It was quite uncanny. There was undoubtedly something unpleasant here.

After the rooms had been visited and each in turn protected by water, Kevin, aided by his priestess, set about ceremoniously cleansing and purifying the building – exorcising it, others would say – invoking the four elements, turning to the north for Earth, the east for Air, the south for Fire and the west for Water.

The ceremony, which lasted half an hour, had just ended when the sky blackened over and there was a violent and most unexpected storm, with howling winds and huge hailstones. This storm, scarcely experienced in the town three quarters of a mile away, lasted ten minutes and then it stopped as suddenly as it had begun.

And then, the entity, whatever it was, left the building. There was an immediate sense of lightness, of calm and peace. It was as though a burden had been lifted. And on their return to work the staff too sensed that some kind of change had been effected. Certainly, the undue succession of severe misfortunes which had so troubled them for three years never again manifested itself.

Kevin is unsure precisely what it was that cast its shadow over Aylesford. Some staff had offered the opinion that they were cursed by gypsies who in 1994 were evicted from the ground when the Post Office decided to build their new unit there. But Kevin inclines to the view that as the building lies on a ley line which runs directly from Lower Kit's Coty, it had been receiving a negative stream of energy which had been responsible for what occurred. Perhaps that is the answer.

Among his more recent ventures Kevin has been called on to visit the *Ross Revenge*, a former Icelandic trawler, which since 1983 has been the second seaborne home of Radio Caroline. From 1967, this pirate radio station had been broadcasting pop music to Britain and Holland from outside territorial waters to the chagrin of the two governments and the delight of millions of young people. Its freebooting days came to an end in 1991 when the *Ross Revenge* ran aground on the Goodwins. The vessel was refloated and towed into Dover for a refit. But then new legislation made it no longer possible to continue the broadcasts. Since then Radio Caroline has operated legally with a restricted licence, broadcasting each weekend via satellite. Some may regret its new respectability but the old pirate still has something from its past for the fact is that ever since Caroline has been in operation aboard this ship, it has had its own ghost.

Right from 1983 when the *Ross Revenge* began its new career as a radio ship, the ghost called 'Sailor Sam' in his sou'wester and oilskins has been sighted in various parts of the vessel. The first time 'Sam' appeared he walked through the mast. Nonsense, some said. Imagination, others added. Booze, yet others opined. But since then 'Sam' has been spotted with some regularity especially in the forepeak, the narrow part of the hold at the front of the ship, as well as on deck, in the galley and the toilet.

It was more the spirit of general curiosity that led to Kevin and Sandie being invited to investigate the mysterious apparition. In June 1999 they paid their first visit to the *Ross Revenge*, at that time anchored off Sheerness. From what they had learned previously it was clear to them that this was no publicity stunt. The telephone calls they made to former members of staff before their arrival and the comments they heard from those aboard dispelled any doubts about the existence of 'Sailor Sam'.

When they talked to the crew and the DJs it was apparent that none of them was especially alarmed by 'Sam'. There were those who were a shade nervous and who would not venture alone into the forepeak but, nevertheless, everyone seemed to believe that he intended no harm. In fact, Peter Moore, the station manager, believed that he appeared to forewarn of trouble. For example, he was certain that in 1987, immediately after the great storm, 'Sam' appeared to DJ Nigel Harris and pointed at the mast. The next day, weakened by the force of the storm, the mast collapsed into the sea. Nigel's view was that the apparition was well disposed to the ship and the crew. Having seen him five times, he was completely pro-'Sam'.

Another of the DJs, Caroline Martin, explained her conviction that in 1989 'Sam' turned up just before the station was forced off the air temporarily by the British and Dutch governments.

In the course of their initial tour of the vessel, the two investigators were first aware of something different, of something in the atmosphere, when they went into the engine room and the forepeak. These were quite unlike any other of the places they inspected. 'Both sent shivers up our spines and it certainly wasn't the static of the transmitters,' Kevin says. 'I can honestly say I have never felt such a strong presence.'

A few weeks later, in August 1999, the two witches joined the ship once more, spending the first night aboard at Southend before being towed the next day to an anchorage off Queensborough, Kent. After an essential briefing on the functioning of the generators and navigation lights, the couple were left alone on board the *Ross Revenge*.

It was on the second evening, as they watched the TV news, that Kevin and Sandie heard the sound of footsteps on the deck above the messroom and galley. Had someone sneaked aboard? Was someone out to make fools of the two observers? They went up on deck.

During the course of the subsequent search, Sandie fore and Kevin aft, the ship's bell in the mess room rang twice. Despite their wide experience of the paranormal both investigators had the powerful and uneasy sense of some presence, just as they had on their previous visit. There was almost a tingle in the air. Then came an overpowering smell of fish and all of the lights went out. The generator had stopped.

Collecting their torch, the couple went down into the haunted forepeak and found the source of the trouble. There was a fuel blockage from the main tank. Without lights, the *Ross Revenge* was now highly vulnerable. This is part of the world's busiest sea lane and it was possible that some vessel – a tanker perhaps – might run down the unlit ship.

While Kevin returned to the forepeak, Sandie stayed up on deck, optimistically flashing torches to alert other ships to their position. Below decks there was still the stink of fish. And no immediate solution to the problem. And both now heard the ship's bell ring again and then came the sound of music from the studio ... *Isadora* played by the Dutch band Illusion. Odd that, an old Seventies number, which they used to play years earlier on the *Mi Amigo*, the original home of Caroline. Odd, too, that that should have been one of Kevin's old favourites. But even odder than anything was the fact that there was no power on board!

It was as he returned to the deck that Kevin saw the figure in the yellow oilskins walk into the transmitter room. He followed the apparition but he was not surprised to find the room empty. Then came a yell from Sandie up on deck. She too had seen 'Sailor Sam'.

Shortly afterwards Kevin and Sandie managed to fill the small generator with diesel. Power was restored and life aboard returned to what might loosely be called normal. Although for the next two days and nights they remained alert there were no other experiences worthy of recording save for the sound of occasional footsteps. 'Sailor Sam' failed to put in a second appearance.

Back home in St Leonards, Kevin and Sandie have pondered the curious case on board the *Ross Revenge*. Why, they wondered, does 'Sailor Sam' usually show himself only when broadcasting begins? Why, when the *Ross Revenge* was off the air in 1991 and part of 1992, did he never appear? Why on Easter Sunday 1992, the day when broadcasting began again legally, did he put in an appearance? What does seem to be the case is that he responds to broadcasting. Or rather that he is activated, given some kind of boost, an electrical charge, when the transmitters are turned on. There does appear to be a connection between electrical energy and the raising of an otherwise dormant spirit. Nevertheless, on the occasion when Kevin and Sandie saw him, there was no power, the generator had failed, and so this presents a further puzzle. At least, there was no power through the normal channels though there was enough from some unidentified source to activate the music in the studio.

And who is this dormant spirit? In its time as a trawler there were two fatal accidents aboard the *Ross Revenge*. In one a sailor became entangled in the fishing nets and was pulled overboard and lost. A second crew member died in a fire in the forepeak. One of these it would seem is the ghost of the *Ross Revenge*, raised by the sheer strength of some energy source.

The Carlyons continue their work, responding to the concerns of the many people who call upon them with a variety of psychic conundrums. They remain convinced that much paranormal activity is rooted in surges of energy, that from these spring many of the seemingly incomprehensible phenomena which so disturb us. As for the *Ross Revenge*, they will undoubtedly return there to investigate further the case of 'Sailor Sam'.

7

The Bromley Poltergeist

One of the most sensational of all poltergeist cases, significant for its curious location, its duration and its violence, occurred in Bromley. It is further remarkable in that the three men who were subjected to such a prolonged and alarming series of attacks decided to keep an account of events and these, along with the records made during investigations carried out by members of the Society for Psychical Research, make for fascinating reading.

The disturbances occurred over an unusually prolonged two-year period on the Grove Park allotments, mainly in the two sheds of the Kentish Garden Guild which was run by three men. This was no mammoth business enterprise. The two adjoining sheds with their corrugated iron roofs and their barbed wire fences were perhaps typical of what one might expect of such a small enterprise set on waste ground among housing estates.

Alfred Taylor, a 78 year old pensioner keeping himself active, used to order whatever was necessary each Thursday and on Sunday mornings he and his two colleagues, Tony Elms and Clifford Jewiss, sold the various items to other allotment holders. It was on one of those Sunday mornings, 26th April 1973, that the first curious incident occurred. This was a day on which Taylor felt that Elms was upset about something. It is worth bearing that in mind. But of course there was never anything to tie the 50 year old Elms (or, indeed, either of the others) into the disturbances, nothing to suggest with any sense of certainty that his mental or psychic state gave some kind of impetus to the succession of incredible happenings at Grove Park.

What happened was out of the blue. The men were in the trading shed when some powder suddenly hit the ceiling. They all looked at it. Kids up to some mischief? Some sort of prank? That was certainly Clifford Jewiss's first thought. Then a small pewter jug on a cupboard shelf suddenly shot across the floor. Even then no one quite took in what was happening. You can buy all sorts of tricks in joke shops. But after Jewiss picked up the jug and put it in a box with a plastic lid they had cause to think again. For the jug was on the floor once more. And the lid of the box was still in place. Matter cannot pass through matter. Anybody knows that. But the jug ...?

Over the following weeks there was a succession of inexplicable happenings. Out of the bin of Growmore fertiliser came fountains of pellets, hitting the ceiling, sometimes showering onto customers. On one occasion a 7lb weight sailed off the scales and round Alf Taylor's head.

Sometimes all manner of items left their places one after another, though no one ever saw them take off. But they watched them, in Taylor's words, 'going round the hut like skittles.' None of the men could understand what was really happening. They tried sometimes to persuade themselves that they were victims of some kind of elaborate hoax but they could not really be convinced of this for the whole exhibition – that is quite a good description of what they were observing so regularly – was too complex to be the result of human agency. Objects were acting as though they had a life of their own.

And this was so damaging to business. It was proving to be extremely costly. Bottles were unscrewed and their contents were poured out on the floor of the shed. The taps of tubs of liquid Maxicrop were turned on. More than 1 cwt of Growmore pellets was lost from the storage bins and remarkably it seemed as if human hands had scooped them out for on the surface of the remaining pellets in one of the tubs there were the impressions of fingers. But no one could easily get at the bins without being seen. How could these be human hands?

It was too the general nuisance, the rather spiteful nature of some of the tricks, that upset the men. Money was taken from one of their cars and later coins fell from the ceiling. Other coins fastened inside plastic bags fell out of their own accord. When Tony Elms was about to drink coffee out of a mug the contents escaped somehow and were replaced with fertiliser.

Elms was a frequent target. He was to say later: 'It frightened me. I've seen a half-ton bag of fertiliser move. The whole building would shake sometimes. Money would fly about and I've seen 7lb bags of fertiliser move from the shelf and hit customers.' There was an occasion when the men had to abandon business before 1pm, the usual closing time, because the objects were moving as fast as they were replaced.

One of the customers, pensioner George Bentley, recalled: 'One time some money disappeared and the next thing I knew a 10p coin fell into a cup of tea I was drinking. Another time I went into the shed to buy a 7lb bag of Growmore. I asked for it and I saw it lift off the shelf, float across and burst open on the counter. There were some right queer goings on and a lot of us saw them.'

The success of the business was undoubtedly imperilled by the manic activities of the poltergeist. Something had to be done. It was Elms who asked the advice of an unspecified group of either churchmen or white magicians. Following their advice he carried out a DIY exorcism alone in the darkness of one of the sheds. Outside, the others could hear bangings so loud that they feared that the walls would collapse. Nine times the heavy iron door swung open as if subjected to massive blows. At the end Tony Elms came out, his head cut and his hand heavily bruised.

But the exorcism – did it work? When the men went back on the Saturday evening to prepare for the next day's sales, the interior of the shed looked 'as if it had been hit by a bomb'. The goods were all thrown off the shelves and circled them in constant motion. All over the walls, on all of the surfaces in the sheds, on chairs, benches, tubs and bins, the sign of the cross was scratched, painted, shaped in drawing pins and drawn. Two large planks (5'6") which had been used to barricade the sheds vanished completely one day. The next day when Taylor and

Elms arrived at the allotments, there were the missing planks arranged in the shape of a cross. It seemed a conscious mockery of Tony Elms and his attempt to exorcise the spirit that so plagued him and his colleagues.

Alf Taylor was attacked away from the premises and in the presence of witnesses in his own home. On another occasion he claimed that he was pushed in Bromley Council Offices. So it did seem that whatever it was that was making life such a misery was not solely active in one place.

In late September 1973 Alf Taylor rang the Society for Psychical Research, asking for help. Manfred Cassirer, Chairman of the Physical Phenomena Committee, and his wife and fellow researcher, Pauline Runnells, met Taylor in his house at Downham and agreed to visit the site. What they saw convinced them that the men were not making up a story. And why should they? The wretched affair was costing them money.

The researchers paid two visits, one in October 1973 and a second in June 1974. The reason for the interval was the reluctance on the part of the three men to delve further into the mysteries. But on their two visits Manfred Cassirer and Pauline Runnells saw the whole remarkable display of tricks and more. They saw security bolts disappear from a window to be rediscovered inside a car outside. In front of them Tony Elms had a saw rammed down his back and his shirt ripped. As they stood inside the building, it was shaken by what seemed to be a series of angry blows.

The number 1659 – a date? a code? – appeared on a wooden panel, the consequence of automatic writing. It looked to be written in blood though had it been analysed perhaps it would have proved to be Maxicrop. And there was more writing and further scrawls – a large question mark; assorted letters of the alphabet; the name of one of Taylor's friends.

On the second visit there were two particularly notable features. There were the usual instances of teleportation. Nothing was safe. A watering can took off; a bottle of ant killer had to be replaced three times on a shelf; wooden planks fell down; a bottle appeared to be suspended in mid-air; and on a shelf what at first sight appeared to be the impression of a child's hand changed imperceptibly into a face yet – and this is the eerie part – the actual movements of the change could not be seen. At first it was a hand, then a face. Then from the counter a rectangular brass object stamped MN dropped onto the floor. But what was it? Where had it come from? None of the men claimed to have seen it before; none of them could interpret MN. It was as though it had come from another world, another dimension.

Then there was another weird manifestation. Before the two researchers arrived a face, of human proportions, took shape on the counter. Made from two chemicals in the shed, its features, outlined in white sulphite, were like a skull. The eyes, nose and mouth were represented by brown Maxicrop. It could not have been made by any of the men. It required skill as well as speed. None of them had either the ability or the time to fashion so curious a piece of artwork. Then before the eyes of all five, allotment holders and observers, the face gradually changed, wore away, wasted, and again no actual movement was seen though all watched its deterioration.

What else? Oh, disappearing car keys; Taylor's missing thermos flask which was found in a carrier bag on Jewiss's motor cycle; £4 of the day's takings lost; a gardening fork returned to the shed after disappearing; fertiliser instead of coffee appearing in a thermos flask; money found inside plastic bags; Elms pushed violently into Cassirer and later almost choked on a flower bulb sticking out of his mouth. What a memorable couple of visits for Cassirer and Runnells.

The visits of the researchers did not call a halt to the activities of the Bromley poltergeist. But stop they did some months later, just as suddenly as they began. The whole wicked, insanely childish behaviour came to an end. It just came to an abrupt halt. 'It all stopped after work on a new block of garages was finished,' according to George Bentley. But how, why, what was it all about? Was it about anything?

Where did it come from, this vandal, this malicious entity? According to one school of thought, poltergeists have their source in the living, in the very personalities who are under siege, and do not spring from the dead. There is the sense of something hidden in a living personality, something waiting to be triggered. But why did it select Tony Elms more frequently than his two colleagues? Was there something in his subconscious self, in his personality? Was there some hidden story, some concealed anger somewhere, some burning resentment? Was he the source or was he simply the target? Did this activity emerge from a deep hidden level? Was it some unsuspected turmoil, some unknown disturbance in either of the other men? Certainly, the affair distressed and mystified all of them. Each of them would have been horrified to think himself the source of this frightening and inexplicable activity.

Others say that poltergeists are intelligences on the loose, intelligences perhaps of humans now dead, and that these leech onto the living, feeding on their disturbed emotional lives. From our internal disorders they gain their sustenance.

But what a mystery it is. What an unnerving mystery.

8

Spirits of the Theatre Royal, Chatham

The Theatre Royal at Chatham, built with all the brio and confidence of the late Victorians in 1899, was the largest theatre outside London, capable of seating up to 3,000 in its plush surroundings. What elegance, what extravagance. Small wonder that it attracted such huge crowds to see Dan Leno and George Robey, Marie Lloyd and Gertie Gitana, and all of the stars of the day up to Harry Secombe and Ken Dodd, Morecambe and Wise. And there were some of the greatest actors and actresses in the land – Robert Donat, Michael Redgrave, Sybil Thorndike, as well as opera and ballet companies from all over the world.

And it all came to nothing. In the Fifties, just like so many of the other great theatres, the Theatre Royal at Chatham closed its doors. It served in several unworthy capacities as warehouse, furniture shop, department store until finally it was in total decline, deserted by all save vagrants and pigeons. It seemed that this beautiful building was destined simply to collapse. And then suddenly there was an upsurge of interest in it. Property dealers homed in on the idea that it could be converted to commercial use. Perhaps it could become a shopping mall. Not so, said others, suddenly and at last aware, after so many years, of the forgotten jewel in their midst. These were the ones who determined to save the old theatre and who aimed to restore it to its former glory. They were ready to fight and work selflessly to put an end to the years of neglect. These restorers – the enthusiasts, volunteers and selfless workers of the Theatre Royal Chatham Trust – have remained loyal to the old theatre.

So too have its ghosts, there since its earliest days, ghosts who stayed with the theatre through two wars as well as through peacetime, and who since the closure in 1955, have remained on site. Today, as preparations go forward for the opening, they still make their presence felt. A woman in a long evening dress has been seen on the second floor; a woman's voice, faint but clear, has been heard; the figure of a man has been spotted in various areas. In several parts of the building, and particularly in the room known as the annexe, there has been significant poltergeist activity. But the stories of the hauntings go back a long way.

Recently Alex Ludlow and Pat Willoughby, who worked in the theatre many years ago, recalled what happened one day in 1943 when they were up in the 'gods', preparing the lighting for a performance. Alex happened to glance over his shoulder and he caught sight of a man, wearing what looked like a duffel coat, standing a few yards away by the staircase. That was wrong, a complete stranger hanging about at that time of day. What on earth was a member of the public doing there?

'Who's that feller there?' Alex asked Pat and together the two young men walked towards the stranger.

'You shouldn't be here, mister!' Pat shouted. 'What're you doing here?'

And with that the stranger took off – straight through the closed doors.

'We turned tail and ran right down,' Alex recalls, 'and we ran into Warren Bennet, the Music Director. He said: "It looks like you two lads have seen a ghost".'

In 1950 Jack Stolton, assistant stage manager at the Chatham Empire, had a similarly odd experience. He needed to borrow some spotlights from the Royal and the fact that the theatre was closed did not present a problem. The staffs of the two theatres were on good terms and he was given the keys to let himself in and out. Jack was to have been accompanied by his stage electrician but he was delayed by other business to attend to at the Empire. The electrician said that he would follow on shortly.

Jack let himself into the empty theatre and made his way to the stage to switch on the lights. When he did so he looked up to the dress circle which was still in shadow. Then he saw a figure there, looking down at him. What the devil was the electrician doing up there?

'Hey, come on down here,' Jack called out. They had no time to waste and he must have felt peeved that his colleague should be messing about where he should not be.

The figure paused and then made towards one of the exits. Jack then left the stage area and made for the foyer where he expected to see the electrician coming down the staircase from the interior of the building. But as he entered the foyer the door from the street opened.

'Sorry I'm late,' the electrician said. 'I was held up longer than I expected.'

Though they looked round the building, for they had no wish to lock anyone inside, they did not come across another soul.

Jack Stolton has no doubt that he had seen one of the ghosts. Perhaps he had. Perhaps he had seen Humphrey, the theatre's best known apparition.

It is said that Humphrey was a trapeze artist who made a serious error in a performance in front of Edward VII. Deeply hurt, humiliated in fact by his failure, he is said to have hanged himself from the dress circle. Unfortunately there is no record of this though there are accounts enough of the so-called Humphrey's regular appearances. Sylvia Flaherty, a former Tiller girl who is also one of the principal initiators of the moves to save the Theatre Royal, says that she saw Humphrey frequently during her appearances at the theatre. Furthermore, Sylvia speaks fondly of him.

'Humphrey is the guardian of the Theatre Royal,' she says, 'and the dress circle is his favourite place. He would sit in one of the front rows and watch a show and if he didn't like it he would get up and walk out. There used to be a heavy glass mirrored door leading from the dress circle to the circle bar and you would hear the door go slam! But there was never a sign of anyone there – no draught, nothing.'

And there is also the story of Humphrey's Curse, a tale that was revived in 1989 on the sudden death of a property developer who was on the point of converting the building into a shopping mall. The theatre was saved at the last minute and there were those who attributed that to the intervention of the theatre's favourite ghost.

Rather less comforting are the poltergeist activities which have been regularly experienced since the Trust began its work. From time to time there are the minor irritations when tools as well as personal possessions go missing only to turn up in other parts of the building. Sometimes electrical equipment stops unaccountably. Roy Phillips, one of the Trust Directors who is also Site Manager, recounts a number of incidents. One day, for example, he turned up at the theatre and found in the foyer work hats and masks that he and three others had been using the previous day. And he has no doubt that they had been put away the night before in their usual cupboard.

'But there have been many incidents of strange, inexplicable happenings within the theatre which I have been aware of,' Roy says. 'I have to say that I was very sceptical with regard to the supernatural, ghosts and that sort of thing, but I am not so sure now.'

One day when the Trust had not long been in possession of the building, Roy was sweeping up the foyer. There was no one else in the theatre at the time. There was a stillness about the place and perhaps, sceptic or no, he began to feel unsure of himself. Roy takes up the story. 'Out of bravado I said: "If there is a spirit here, give me a sign." Immediately there was a crash some 30 feet away from where I was standing as though a ceramic tile had fallen to the floor. I walked towards the area where the sound came from but the floor was completely clear and there were no signs of broken tiles. Laughing, I returned to where I had previously been standing and said, "Well, at least you didn't throw anything at me but I'd still like some proof of your existence." There was immediately another crash as before but much closer this time. When I investigated the area, again there was no evidence of any broken tiles.'

On yet another occasion when he was waiting for some others to turn up, Roy went into the auditorium and put a tape in the music centre. *Phantom of the Opera* – perhaps it was appropriate. As the music swelled Roy walked back into the foyer. And suddenly the music came to a stop. Back he went into the auditorium but when he was within six feet of the music centre the music started up again. Coincidence? A minor bleep with the electrics? Perhaps, but it should be remembered that the malfunctioning of electrical equipment is not unknown when poltergeists are active.

The experiences of some others are distinctly less pleasant, especially in the upstairs room known as the annexe. Here at Christmas 1995 one woman saw the door slam shut and then reopen of its own accord a number of times. Later she felt a slap on the side of her face. On a different occasion, in the same room, another woman felt a hand run gently down her left cheek. And it is in this room that two separate parties of policemen on a 'stakeout' felt unable to continue their duties. The slamming doors and the unaccountable sound of footsteps in the passageway outside unnerved them and they left. And really when the natural laws are broken, when things occur which are contrary to normal expectation, when rationality is turned on its head, who can wonder that fears are roused?

Elsewhere in this great old theatre, in one particular spot in the auditorium, there is sometimes the smell of sweet plug pipe tobacco. Not everyone can smell it but there are enough witnesses to this curious phenomenon. And it is curious for no one has smoked in this building for nearly 50 years. And anyway, who smokes such old-fashioned pipe tobacco these days?

In September 1996 there was a sponsored ghost watch at the Theatre Royal. An internationally acknowledged spiritualist Robin Wimbow, and others, recorded what they saw and heard. What was most reassuring in their report to the Trust members was that in general the spirits in the building approve warmly of what the restorers are doing.

And one supposes that in turn the restorers approve of

Humphrey, for a seat is to be reserved for him in the dress circle on the evening of the first performance. And with Humphrey on their side, how can the restorers fail in their great and imaginative task?

9

Unwelcome Guests

Poltergeists, so often mischievous and malicious, represent one of the most frightening paranormal manifestations. The problem is that we cannot understand them and their frenetic activity, and the ferocious power they so frequently unleash. With the apparition, for example, we can often point to its history. We can say, for example, this is the ghost of a nun who was walled up, of a smuggler who fell off a cliff, of a couple devoted to their own old home and who cannot drag themselves away. But poltergeists are more difficult. Their origins and what it is that they are about are mystifying and frequently frightening, as the case of the Bromley poltergeist described earlier demonstrates.

The Theatre Royal at Margate was long troubled by poltergeist activity. Indeed, this troublesome and irritating ghost has been held responsible for the theatre's closure. Some attributed the activity to Sarah Thorne, the theatre's most successful manager, or to an actor who had been replaced and who purchased a seat in a box where he killed himself during a performance. Or was it some other anonymous and spiteful spirit? Whoever it was, bolted emergency doors; unbolted locked doors after the audiences had left; turned out emergency lights; switched on main lighting during the night; moved scenery and props; turned lights on and off; and shuffled and thudded about the building when it was all but empty. From time to time there were even severe icy blasts in the warmest and most comfortable parts of the building. Such is the sometimes ungovernable and irrational power of the poltergeist.

There are certainly fundamental questions which exercise the minds of those who study the paranormal. Why, such students ask, do poltergeists make so many childish, spiteful, sometimes dangerous attacks? Is it because they are so often the outcome of children's or adolescents' anxieties? Is it because at other times they stem from obsessions and compulsions of older persons? Are we dealing here with repression or other deep-seated emotions? Does some subconscious and abnormal element of the personality promote some physical force? Does the presence in a house of some innocent person or other, a child, say, stir something into action? But why are two different families affected when in turn they occupy the same property? Is there some paranormal violence in the very substance of the dwelling, set off by certain personalities?

Or are there random intelligences, possibly human, probably non-human, which like vampires feed off the living and their disjointed emotions? Certainly this is the explanation, incredible though it may seem, favoured by some of the experts in the field. But these are speculations about an extremely complex problem.

*   *   *   *

What strikes one about the following cases is the very ordinariness of the families involved. Take the Maxteds, a couple with four children, living in the 1960s at 16 Waterdales in Northfleet. They were terrified by weird banging and scraping noises in the night; by doors which were unaccountably found to be locked or unlocked; by lights which were switched off and on. Small wonder that they asked the council to rehouse them, which they did in February 1965.

Before they moved in, the Maxteds' successors, a young tugboat engineer, Eric Essex, and his wife Margaret, were warned by council officers that there had been some unnerving events in the house but the couple were only too glad to find council accommodation. And in any case, they probably thought that their predecessors had made a fuss about nothing. All the same, at their request a local clergyman came to bless the house. No harm in taking precautions, they must have thought, especially as they had two very young children. The Rev Alan Gordon of All Saints, using the Ancient Order of Blessing, said a prayer in each room and made the sign of the cross using holy water.

But within 18 months Eric and Margaret Essex were frantically applying for a transfer. To be fair they had over the months dismissed odd sounds and smells, shrugged their shoulders at the tapping noises and the footsteps. But the uneasy atmosphere had become increasingly worrying. Most of the sounds appeared to come from the front bedroom which they had abandoned and now used as a storeroom, rarely entering it save when absolutely necessary. But they had tried to stick it out.

Then one Sunday night in August 1966, at the end of a week when the smell in the house became overpowering, Eric Essex got out of bed when he thought he heard someone walking up and down the hall. He investigated but finding nothing, returned to bed and fell asleep. Some time later he woke again and heard a high-pitched whistling sound.

'I opened my eyes,' he said, 'and saw an orange pink sort of mist surrounding the figure of a woman standing close to my bed. As far as I could see she had no head. One thing I can clearly remember is that she was wearing a large sash. The whole of the bed was shaking violently. I tried to speak but I just couldn't. All I could do was to lie there until the thing moved off in the direction of the bedroom door where it finally disappeared.'

At last, somewhat recovered, he woke his wife who had slept undisturbed through the whole incident. Within minutes they and the children were on their way to relatives. And they had no intention of going back to 16 Waterdales.

If the council were not immediately sympathetic, then others certainly confirmed the stories of the Essexes and the Maxteds. Next door at No 14, Mrs Margaret Harrison told of how she had heard noises and had talked to Mr and Mrs Essex about them. She was certain that there was something genuinely wrong at the neighbouring house. Her five year old son had sometimes wakened up crying and screaming for no apparent reason. One night when Mrs Harrison had gone into his room he had been 'absolutely frozen to the touch.' Eventually she had refused to stay in the house alone when her husband was working in Scotland and had taken her children to stay with relatives. After his experience Eric Essex recalled something similar to what Mrs Harrison had mentioned: 'My left arm, the one nearest to the apparition, was absolutely frozen, and it stayed cold for the rest of the day.'

Mrs Diane Alice, who had formerly lived at 14 Waterdales, admitted that she had been frightened when awakened at three o'clock by what sounded like footsteps from next door. But then she had recalled that council officials had explained some years earlier that ceilings put in the roofs of the houses when they were rebuilt after bombing in the Second World War would exaggerate any sound. Once over her fright, she decided that the noise must have come from birds in the roof. But now she was inclined to doubt that conclusion.

Of course stories like these, wherever they occur, are godsends to the press. In September 1966 Dick Moore and Bill Garland, two very young *Kent Messenger* reporters, and Malcolm Bennett, an equally young financial accounts clerk, spent a night in the now empty 16 Waterdales. On going into the house they immediately noticed the heavy musty smell that is most usually associated with properties left vacant over several months. But No 16 had been empty for only a few days.

They decided to base themselves in the bedroom in which Eric Essex had seen his headless woman. The early part of their watch was uneventful. Then, some time shortly after midnight, the room temperature suddenly fell. They noted that cigarette smoke swirled in a draught which appeared to exist in the corner of the room where Mr Essex claimed to have seen the apparition. Yet the windows and doors were tightly shut. After a minute or so, the draught went and the cigarette smoke followed its customary course towards the ceiling.

During the next hour the three men heard rustling noises.

Then it seemed that something was sliding along the floor although they could see nothing which gave rise to this. When Dick Moore summoned up courage and went to investigate outside the room he heard the sound of creaking floorboards coming from the lower flight of stairs.

After 1.30 am there were no further disturbances. Nevertheless, at times during what must have seemed an endless night, the men noticed pressure on their eardrums and their faces felt hot whilst their hands and feet were freezing cold. The report in the newspaper made no attempt to disguise the relief they felt when their night-long vigil came to an end. None of them would have volunteered to stay there on his own. Dick Moore wrote: 'Although we did not see anything during the night, from the moment we entered the house I had the feeling we were not entirely alone.'

It was said that during the war a man had died from shrapnel wounds almost on the doorstep of 16 Waterdales. But does that explain the headless woman with the sash? Then it has to be recalled that apparitions are distinctly different from poltergeists. It must be asked therefore if this property did not house both kinds of manifestation.

The haunting of 16 Waterdales seems inexplicable yet it is similar to so many other hauntings. In 1969, for instance, in a house in Imperial Road in Gillingham, lights switched themselves off and on and furniture moved apparently of its own accord. In Sandgate, the little seaside suburb of Folkestone, there were reports of a shop where pieces of furniture changed their position overnight.

* * * *

In another case in Northfleet in the same period the groundsman of the Mid Kent Golf Club was driven from his home at 40 Overcliffe after tappings at his bedroom window and the sound of shuffling feet inside the house. In the tense frightening atmosphere he was unable to sleep soundly. Something always seemed to be going on or, perhaps worse still, it seemed as though something unspecified was about to happen. On one occasion he woke and as he sat up in bed he saw the doors of a built-in cupboard opening and shutting of their own will. It was all too much for him. Principally, it was all too much because there was no rationale to what was happening. This is the real problem with poltergeist activity. It defies explanation. It so often defies the laws of nature for things do not move of their own accord.

At Dartford in January 1977 the district council was worried that people would be deterred from occupying one of its smart semi-detached houses in Ruskin Grove because of 'things that go bump in the night'. A family of six, the Robertsons, had had to be rehoused. And it was especially sad because since they had moved into the house in 1975 the Robertsons had spent a considerable amount on furnishings and decoration. But by late 1976 they were forced to quit. Barry Robertson, a railway guard, said that they had lost everything. They had sold or burned most of the furniture: they could not bear the thought of keeping it.

The strange events had begun almost as soon as they moved in. Although he said nothing to his family, on removal day Barry Robertson saw a blurred outline at the top of the stairs. 'It was as if something was looking down the stairs at me,' he said. In the next months three of the children complained of things moving in the night. Claire, the four year old, spoke of a boy, rather like her eleven year old brother Philip, who came to her bedside and touched her face. Nine year old Mark screamed one night and when his parents ran into the bedroom he appeared to be pushing something away. But on other occasions the parents saw bedclothes moving of their own accord; they saw piles of washing moving in the air; there were potatoes thrown from the rack round the kitchen before shooting up to the ceiling. There were times when brass ornaments were knocked off the edge of a wall unit by an ash tray; there was the occasion when the cat went wild trying to get out of the room and the night when the border collie Bess could not settle but instead growled and barked at the corner of the sitting room. Furniture and ornaments moved for no apparent reason; a rocking horse belonging to the children moved from one side of a bedroom to another while a family friend looked on in horror; and then Mr Robertson's mother refused to continue baby-sitting for them after hearing footsteps upstairs across one of the children's bedrooms. She knew that there was no adult upstairs at the time.

The family was understandably terrified. They called in a local cleric to bless the house and he was satisfied when he left that he had cleared the house of whatever it was that ailed it. 'There is no doubt that the family encountered something strange and frightening,' he said. 'So far as I am concerned whatever was wrong is no longer there. All is well now.'

But after some days the disturbances resumed and the Robertsons were rehoused. Since then the house has been regularly occupied and the tenants have had no sign of any poltergeist activity. Was this then a consequence of some child's inner turmoil? Did the events which frightened each and every member of the family spring unconsciously from the anxieties of one of its members? Were there at that time unrecognised tensions within the family?

Or was it some unfettered intelligence who chose at random to batten onto an unsuspecting family?

10

Life After Death on the Goodwins?

'The Goodwins, I think they call the place; a very dangerous flat – and fatal – where the carcasses of many a tall ship lie buried.' This is how Shakespeare describes those constantly shifting banks of sand which so terrified the sailors of his age. Even so, many centuries earlier, before the Romans and the Saxons, before the Danes and the Normans, the Great Ship Swallower was known for its treachery and many a sailor, careless perhaps or lacking respect, one might say, or merely ignorant, lost his life in these unforgiving waters. But the Goodwin Sands needed to be negotiated for seamen seeking the Downs, that stretch of sheltered water off the coast of Kent. At one time in those distant days as many as 200 ships might be found at anchor off Deal and Ramsgate. Small wonder, then, with so much traffic that there have been so many tragedies hereabouts and small wonder, too, that ghost ships are spotted here from time to time.

One summer's day in 1967, Peter and Kim Hinckley, with their sons John and David, were sailing off Deal in their yacht, *Grey Seal*. At midday they noticed the sky to the east beginning to darken. What had started out as a beautiful day was suddenly threatening as though a storm were brewing. Several hundred yards away, under glowering skies, they noticed a dense mist which oddly enough looked to be confined to a narrow, specific area where the sea was churning up into huge waves. What the Hinckleys saw was a violent storm in a quite tight area. It was an abnormal weather feature which both intrigued and rather alarmed the family and they were drawn to the rail of the *Grey Seal*, so remarkable did the scene appear to be. Outside of the misty, turbulent stretch of sea the surface of the water still remained calm and the sun continued to shine. It was bizarre. For ten minutes the family waited as though they knew that something unusual was about to occur.

And then came an explosion, though it was not obvious why for it came from the mist-shrouded waters. Then, out of the slowly clearing mist, there emerged a sailing ship, struggling through the raging sea. It became increasingly clear to the observers that the ship was in severe distress for it was listing badly. Through binoculars the Hinckleys saw sailors jumping off the ship into the boiling waters. Were they in the middle of a film shoot? They edged *Grey Seal* closer and it soon became apparent that this was no costume drama. That was no mock-up of an early 19th century ship and the men in the water were not film extras. It was a solid craft and the men in the water were terrified, swimming for their lives. And then as *Grey Seal* came closer the mist began to dissipate, the sun shone through, the waters calmed. And the men in the water simply faded and of the ship there was not a sign. In seconds the sky and the sea were restored to summer.

Bewildered at the scene enacted in front of them, the Hinckleys made enquiries of the Coastguard Service. There had been no reports of vessels in distress. And no, there had been no film shoots in the area.

The family members were agreed that the ship they saw had been called *Snipe*. Their later researches, they said, showed that a gun-brig, *Snipe*, went down in this area in 1807. But in fact *Snipe* was in service well after that, ending her days in 1846 as a mooring light at Chatham.

Had the Hinckleys made an error about the ship's name? After all there was much more to see in the few minutes in which they believed themselves playing a part in a real-life adventure. Certainly the facts as related by this family of four do not tally with the records. On the other hand, that four people should make a claim to have seen a ghost ship invites one's interest. So this account ought to be treated with caution but certainly not lightly dismissed.

There are two vessels which really do haunt the Goodwins. One of them is the *Toogoo*, a two-masted Estonian schooner, on her way from Calais to South Shields on Saturday, 1st November 1919. Foundering in mountainous seas, she sent out desperate distress calls. At 10.45 pm the North Deal lifeboat crew responded to guns and rockets and, despite hurricane winds, managed to put to sea. They finally struggled to the stricken boat at 2 am. The *Toogoo* was breaking up fast and six of the crew were huddled together in the rigging, holding on in the fiercest of freezing winds and lashed by violent waves. Two others were hanging on amidships. One of these was the master's wife. Just as the lifeboat was manoeuvring into position, a wave more ferocious than the others hit the *Toogoo* and she was toppled over on her broadside. Those who had sought to save themselves by clinging to the rigging were flung into the water and none of these was saved, all of them washed away before the lifeboatmen's eyes. As was the master's wife who, in the seconds before being snatched into the sea, was heard to utter a terrible shriek, a shriek of such terror that it could be heard above all other sounds.

The *Toogoo* has not been seen since the night she foundered on the Goodwin Sands along with three other ships. But at times, when the seas run high and the tearing winds seem to threaten even the sturdiest craft, there can be heard, above all other sounds, the unearthly shriek of a woman.

One phantom ship which has been sighted on the Goodwins is the SS *Violet* which went down with the loss of all hands in the early hours of Tuesday, 6th January 1857. The *Violet*, a paddle steamer, which belonged to the Royal Dover Steam Packet Company, made regular crossings between Dover and Ostend, carrying passengers and mail. Late on the Monday evening she left Ostend in the most fearful conditions, sailing into a storm with driving winds and thick blankets of snow which had raged in these waters and right up the coast of Britain for the past week.

Off the Durham coast five ships had already been lost and it was the same tale elsewhere. In some areas of the country, so ferocious were the gales that even houses were blown down.

Such conditions, however, did not deter Captain Lyne of the *Violet* who believed that he might take advantage of the storm winds and complete the passage from Ostend more quickly than usual. In any event he calculated that the storm would blow itself out. Even so only one passenger had dared risk the crossing. Others booked to make the trip to Dover elected to wait until the storms abated.

At about 2 am the crewmen on the North Sand Head lightship saw the *Violet* through a thick swirl of snow. It was apparent that she was in extremes of danger, approaching if not already into the Sands. At once the lightship set off rockets and fired signal guns and the steamer *Aid*, with the Ramsgate lifeboat in tow, responded. Within an hour of the first alert, the rescuers reached the area indicated to them by the lightship but in the snowstorm and the impenetrable dark they could find no sign of any craft or of any members of her crew. She had gone down in the driving snow squalls.

When daylight broke, part of the mast sticking up in the water revealed the *Violet*'s position on the southern edge of the Goodwins. Later, at low tide, what little remained of the 300 ton vessel sat upright on the sand. Her funnel had gone and the decks, the bulkheads and the cabin doors had all been wrenched off although the tops of the paddle wheels were still visible.

The lifeboatmen who had stuck to their task throughout the night now came across the *Violet*'s battered lifeboat and three members of her crew lashed to it. There were no other bodies found.

A crew of 17, one passenger and a Post Office mail guard were lost, leaving 16 widows and 43 fatherless children. The mail guard, William Mortleman, a father of ten, had struggled to release the mailbags from the depository, dragging them from their berths and setting them adrift so that they were not lost. It was yet another act of selflessness and attention to duty that marked that awful night. The mail bags were all ultimately recovered.

This was said not to be an inevitable disaster. Had Captain Lyne decided to delay his departure on one of the worst passages imaginable in the North Sea his ship would not have been lost. But perhaps the real error was in mistaking the positions of the lights which marked the Sands. It was suggested that the *Violet* caught a glimpse of one of the floating Gull Streams lights on the east and mistook it for the South Sand Head and shaped her course north-west. It was a mistake that other experienced skippers had made.

In January 1947 George Goldsmith Carter, a historian of the Goodwins, was serving on the lightship. He saw a steamer in severe weather approaching the Sands and in desperate straits. Then, just as if a thick net curtain had been drawn over the scene, the ship vanished in blinding snow. Nevertheless the lightship fired rockets and radioed shore, calling out the Ramsgate lifeboat. But she found nothing.

Carter had spotted the *Violet.*

One hesitates to introduce one of the best known ships in ghostly lore. This is the *Lady Luvibond*, which according to the story – and take care, well known as it is there may be some doubt about this story – sank with all hands on 14th February 1748. Some say that it was only to be expected. She went down because the captain had his wife on the ship. It was unlucky to have a woman on board and certainly many sailors in those days stuck to that particular prejudice or superstition, call it what you will.

The story is that Captain Simon Peel had just married and was determined to take his new bride down to Oporto on his next trip. And so he brought her on board and there were great celebrations on the three-master as she sailed down the Thames and out to sea. But they had not gone far when, approaching the Goodwins, the mate at the helm deliberately ran the vessel aground. Apparently he was mad with love for his captain's wife and jealous that his rival had taken her from him. In his rage he drove the *Lady Luvibond* into the Sands and all hands were lost. Some accounts tell of a struggle aboard and lives lost before the mate, single-handed, wrested control of the ship from Captain Peel and took those who remained alive to their death.

The *Lady Luvibond* appears, they say, every 50 years. And exactly 50 years to the day in 1798, according to reports, the phantom ship was so close that she was almost run into by the *Edenbridge*, whose captain reported hearing sounds of celebration. Then in 1848, after another 50 years, longshoremen at Deal are alleged to have seen the ship. It was clearly in distress and the lifeboat set out to rescue her. But once they were out on the Goodwins, there was no vessel in distress nor any wreckage nor were there sailors fighting for their lives in the raging waters.

In 1898 there was no sign of the *Lady Luvibond* though there are disputed claims that she was seen in 1948. In February 1998 people flocked to the shore to see if they could catch sight of the stricken ghost ship but despite an all-night vigil the watchers were disappointed.

The problem with this much loved phantom is that the story is without solid foundation. How is it known that there was a fight on the ship if all hands were lost? And there is no record in the newspapers of the day of the ship's loss. Lloyd's Register does not survive pre-1764 and so there is no help from that reliable source. But Lloyd's List has no record of a ship of this name nor is there in the List any reference to any vessel being wrecked on the Goodwin Sands in either February or March 1748. It might be, of course, that the *Lady Luvibond* sailed without being insured, which would explain the absence of her name from Lloyd's records. There are those too who dislike the idea of cyclical ghosts, that is ghosts who appear on regular dates, sometimes once a year or in the case of the *Luvibond*, every 50 years. After all, how do they know the date? How do they fit in leap years? And anyway, wasn't the *Luvibond* sunk in the time of to the Old Style calendar so that 'the date' should really be several days later?

But these are quibbles, for isn't the *Lady Luvibond* one of Kent's favourite ghost ships? How one hopes that there really is a *Lady Luvibond* which returns every 50 years. Perhaps it will be cleared up in 2048.

11

Sailors Home from the Sea

Can an emotion be so intensely felt that it causes a profound psychic disturbance, so that an apparition of someone living or very recently dead can appear to cross whole oceans and land masses? As a recent example of this kind of occurrence, some will attest to the fact that they saw Terry Waite, special envoy of the Archbishop of Canterbury, in the cathedral at a time when he was a hostage in Beirut. How can that be accounted for? Did he yearn so deeply for the place? Was it always on his mind? Presumably it was, but plenty of others have yearned deeply for distant places. Perhaps there is an especially potent psychic power in some people that enables this to happen. And perhaps this also helps to explain the following two accounts.

There is no doubt from the report of the nightmarish sinking of HMS *Victoria* in 1893 off Tripoli that many of the drowning men underwent a terrifying experience. Was it the intensity of their terror in these circumstances that led to one of them appearing in his home in Broadstairs on the day of the disaster and at the very moment of death?

The Times carried a series of graphic reports of the disaster. They tell how, manoeuvring off Tripoli, at five o'clock in the afternoon of 22nd June 1893, the Admiral's flagship, HMS *Victoria*, was in collision with HMS *Camperdown*. Within 15 minutes the *Victoria* sank in 80 fathoms with the loss of 370 officers and men. The scenes were horrific. As the ship went down hundreds of crew members desperately fought for their lives in the water. 'Another moment and a new horror was visited

74

upon the struggling men,' says *The Times*. 'The powerful engine, deep down in the heart of the ship and enclosed in the watertight compartments, kept throbbing and working, and the formidable steel flanges of the twin screws whirled round and round, at first high up in space and then gradually they came nearer and nearer to the surface of the water until the ship descended in the midst of the mass of human beings struggling for life, and then as it disappeared the suction increased until it became a perfect maelstrom, at the bottom of which these deadly screws were moving like circular knives, gashing and killing the poor creatures who had battled vainly for life ... Shrieks were heard and then the waves and the foam were reddened by the blood of the hundreds of victims. Arms, legs wrenched from bodies, headless trunks, were tossed out of the vortex to linger on the surface for a few moments and then disappear.'

The Times went on to report that Admiral Sir George Tryon, whose error had been responsible for the catastrophe, had stayed on the bridge to the end when the ship turned over.

Back at Broadstairs on that same afternoon Mrs Kingston, whose son was an Able Seaman aboard the *Victoria*, was startled by what she thought was a gas explosion. Well, she told herself, you were always hearing about such things these days. But this was only a fleeting thought and Mrs Kingston had no time to pull herself together for there in the corner of her bedroom was a strange orange glow. What next? Was it fire then? No, certainly not, for within seconds there was a change of colour and more oddly a change in its very shape for now it stretched upwards and then, of a sudden, assumed what undoubtedly was a vague human form. And then the details filled in, the clothes of a sailor, the features of a young man. Mrs Kingston's own son stood before her in her home. But how?

The young man smiled. 'I'm safe now, mother. Don't worry. I'll see you soon,' he told her. Odd, wasn't it? Strange, that incident in a Broadstairs house on 22nd June 1893.

And some days later, on 3rd July, Mrs Kingston received a telegram from the Admiralty expressing regret that her son had been drowned with his ship, HMS *Victoria*.

It is of course very rare that ghosts actually interact with the living in the manner described above in the case of Seaman Kingston. The occasions when ghosts speak are infrequent but there are some recorded instances. At Chartwell, for example, Randolph Churchill allegedly held a lengthy conversation with his late father, Sir Winston. At Canterbury in 1705, Mrs Bargrave is said to have spent two hours in the presence of a friend, Mrs Veal, who, unknown to her, had died the previous day in Dover.

In the following account the interchange was brief. Nevertheless, it falls into that category where there is some interaction. Did the dead boy, thousands of miles away from those who loved him, in some way manage to project his spirit across the Atlantic to the house where his mother had been recently working?

Pick up this story in Greenwich late in the evening of 8th September 1866. There had been a knock at the door of a most respectable house and the housemaid, Emma Mann, did not like such late callers. Eleven o'clock at night was no time to be knocking at doors and expecting answers. Who on earth could it be? This time of night folk ought to be in bed. Such was Emma Mann's opinion as she made her way downstairs and across the hallway.

The mistress was up in bed just as you would expect of any Christian soul and if the master was not yet abed, well at least she had no doubt he was doing something worthwhile in his study. Emma laid the candle on the floor as she struggled with bolts and locks and eventually the door was open. She did not know whether to be surprised for she had not known who to expect. But there on the step was a sailor lad. Couldn't be more than 17, 18, she thought, scrutinising him in the dim light of the candle. Handsome young chap, though, even if he was a bit on the pale side. And would you believe it, he had no shoes on him.

'Mrs Cooper,' said the lad speaking up in a clear voice. 'I wish to see Mrs Cooper.'

'There's no one here of that name,' Emma told him. 'We haven't no Mrs Cooper here.'

He had put his hand to his brow as though in distress. 'What shall I do?' he asked. 'And *you* also are strange to me.'

At which the young sailor turned on his heel and went off into the dark.

Emma closed and bolted the door and turning saw the mistress in her wrapover at the top of the stairs. 'Who was that, Emma?' she asked.

'Just a sailor lad, mum. Said he was looking for a Mrs Cooper. I told him there wasn't no Mrs Cooper here.'

'What did he look like?' Mrs Hammond asked.

When Emma told her that he was pale, Mrs Hammond shook her head. No, it could not be Tom Potter. He was anything but pale. Tom was ruddy complexioned, always fresh and healthy, young Tom. And anyway, Tom was away in the West Indies. Still, she was uneasy and she sought out her husband.

'Tom Potter at the door?' Mr Hammond said. 'Ridiculous.'

'I shouldn't have got up but I heard the voice. I was sure it was Tom.'

Mr Hammond shook his head. How could it be Tom?

'But he asked for Mrs Cooper,' his wife persisted. 'We don't know any Mrs Cooper.' And then she added, 'He was in navy uniform, just like Tom. It must have been him. But why did he not ask for us?'

'More like one of his shipmates. Tom's mentioned that his mother was here last year and has assumed she is still here. This young fellow's on leave and Tom's asked him to look her up. Perhaps the chap made a mistake with the name.'

That might be the answer, Mrs Hammond grudgingly allowed. But before she fell asleep she determined that the next day she would try to get to the bottom of this matter.

The Hammonds had good reason to be concerned. They were devout Catholics, living in a very comfortable house, St Mary's Lodge, on Croom's Hill in Greenwich. They had moved in there eight years earlier, in 1858, glad that their home was near to the local church, St Mary, Star of the Sea, and even more delighted that the house next door to them was a Catholic boys' orphanage run by Dr William Todd, a distinguished theologian. In their eight years at the Croom's Hill house, the Hammonds, still relatively young and active, became deeply involved in the affairs of the orphanage. Mrs Hammond went there daily and so encouraging and helpful was she to the boys – there were about 60 of them – that many of them came to regard her as their mother. The Hammonds were allowed to nominate boys for places at the home from worthy families which were in reduced circumstances. One such boy was Thomas Potter whose father had died when he was about ten years old and whose mother was finding life a struggle. She was concerned that her son would never have a chance to do well in life. He was a lively enough boy but there was no one to take him in hand in Camberwell. He was a perfect candidate for the boys' home to which he was introduced by Mrs Hammond in 1860.

Tom Potter turned out to be a good, decent lad. Not too perfect, of course. He was in boyish scrapes from time to time but nothing to worry anyone. In fact, he seemed just right for a place in the Navy. And so, on 12th December 1863, Tom Potter, just under 5 feet in height, joined his first ship, HMS *Fisgard*, as Boy 26. Just the place for a lively lad they might have thought. Lad of spirit, he couldn't do better than join the Navy.

But he hated it. The Royal Navy, which the Hammonds and Dr Todd might have thought would suit young Tom to a tee, just did not suit him at all. At the end of his first voyage he ran away as did three other first-time sailors.

And Tom ran straight back to the home and to Dr Todd and the Hammonds. But Tom, they said, with all the collective patience they could muster, it is a fine career for a young fellow like you. Give it another chance, do.

He could see their point. Good career for a chap who stuck in, who did his best. And the first trip was always a trial for young boys. The old sailors plagued them but it was all in the spirit of fun, of comradeship. He would see that when he went back.

But the punishment for desertion was the cat. He couldn't face that. The cat, the stripes across his back. He'd seen a man punished so in front of all the crew. He was a big strong carpenter and he had fainted with the pain.

'Well, then, Tom, I'll see what can be done about that,' Dr Todd told him.

And he did. And Tom went back to sea, promising to stick it out, to give the sailor's life another chance.

In December 1865, now 16 years old, Tom came home on leave from HMS *Impregnable*. He had settled down and had done well. He was to join his new ship, HMS *Doris*, with a complement of 477, in early January. It was a good leave. His mother had been taken on temporarily as an extra maid over the holiday period. It was from here, at St Mary's Lodge, that Tom said goodbye to her. He was bound for Jamaica where there had been civil disturbances. And he was now classified for men's service, signed on for ten years.

And in bed, after the mysterious call from the sailor lad, Mrs Hammond remained uneasy. Had Tom run away again, she wondered. She suggested that to her husband who dismissed the idea out of hand. Hadn't they had a letter from the boy only two or three days ago? And hadn't that been sent from Jamaica?

But Mrs Hammond could not get it out of her head that this was Tom and that he was in some sort of trouble. She sent for Dr Todd who had some photographs of the boy. He showed them to Emma. Yes, that was him, she told them. That's the lad who was at the door last night.

Perhaps he was in Camberwell with his mother. That was a possibility. So off they went, Dr Todd and the Hammonds. But no, Tom's mother had not seen her son since Christmas. But they did note her change of name. She had recently remarried. She was now Mrs Cooper. And that was the name the sailor lad had asked for the previous evening.

The solution, if that is what it was, came a week or so later in a letter from the Admiralty. Seaman Tom Potter had fallen from the masthead of HMS *Doris* on 24th July. He had been taken to Port Royal Hospital where on 6th September he had died of his injuries. During his last days he had called frequently for his mother. She had written to tell him of her remarriage.

On the evening of 8th September 1866, Emma Mann had

grumbled her way to the front door of the Hammonds' house where only months before Tom Potter's mother had worked as a temporary maid. She had spoken to a boy who had died in Jamaica two days earlier. And he had spoken to her.

Perhaps it is worth suggesting that this projection over such distances almost at the time of death is the consequence of a deep wish, a longing, and which certain personalities can achieve as a consequence of some powerful psychic quality. That is not to say that they are aware of any power that enables them, merely on the strength of their yearning, to make appearances far beyond their present physical situation. Certainly, Terry Waite was unaware that he was seen in Canterbury Cathedral. But sometimes both living and dead can most certainly appear simultaneously in places far apart.

12

A Dartford Mystery

The ability of the dead or dying to appear before friends or relatives plays a part in a strange story from 18th century Kent. It was approaching midnight on 27th November 1779 and Miles Andrews had already retired to bed at his house in Dartford, for he was feeling under the weather and had left his partner's wife, Mrs Pigou, to look after his houseful of guests. Andrews, MP for Bewdley and owner of the Dartford gunpowder mills, the greatest in England, was extremely wealthy, a man whose great entertainments and galas attracted all of fashionable London, all that was rich and all that was dissolute. This evening's gathering at his house near the present Walnut Tree Avenue was as noisy and boisterous as ever. It would be more so on the Sunday when his great friend Thomas, Lord Lyttleton, had promised to come to join the party. Andrews and Lyttleton had for years been great companions. They had participated in 'many an orgy and in great profligacy'.

Andrews was suddenly roused some time between 11 and 12 o'clock. The bed curtains were thrown back and as he sat up he was aware of a figure at the bed end. There was someone standing there wearing a nightcap and gown. Was it Lyttleton? It surely was. What the devil was the fellow doing here at this time of night? What was he up to, decked out in this manner? But there came no answer to those questions. There was simply a grim voice telling him that all was over. All over? What on earth ... was this another of Lyttleton's tricks, one of his customary foolish pranks? Andrews was poorly, in no mood for such frivolity. He leaned over the side of the bed, picked up a slipper and threw it at the figure. But there was no one there. Lyttleton had vanished.

Mystified, yet still convinced that this was some kind of trick being played on him, Andrews climbed out of bed and searched the room. He called for his manservant and together they searched the adjoining rooms. Soon enough the guests downstairs were enlisted into the hunt for Lyttleton. All of the rooms in the house were gone through and then the out-buildings were inspected by servants called from their beds. This was infuriating, Andrews said. When they found Lyttleton, he was not to be given a bed. If he thought it a joke then he would have a smile on the other side of his face. Either he would sleep in the stables or he would have to find an inn somewhere in Dartford. Certainly tonight he would not sleep under Andrews' roof.

But in the morning there was still no sign of his lordship. It was Mrs Pigou who went off to London later in the day and heard the news. His lordship was dead. He had died the previous evening at Pit Place. But she knew of all the fuss there had been in the night at Dartford, when everyone was out searching for Lyttleton. It was unaccountable. What on earth had occurred? She sent an express rider with the news down to Dartford. At 4 pm Andrews heard that his friend was dead. He had died at about midnight the previous day. The shock of this information caused Andrews to faint, unable to accept what he was hearing. Had his friend not appeared at his bedside at that time, at the very hour when he was alleged to have died? And had they not once in jest, he remembered, promised each other that the first of them to die would appear to the other?

But this ghostly visit was not the only mystery of this strange story. In London something had disturbed the peace of Thomas, Lord Lyttleton three days earlier. Was it a dream or a ghost? Was the warning of imminent death that he received simply one of the frequent and horrific dreams from which he suffered? Or did the ghost of a woman, described variously as one of his several wronged mistresses – Mrs Amphlett or Miss Kay or Mrs Dawson or one of many others – appear at the end of his bed and say to him: 'Prepare to die'?

Did he dream that he had answered, 'I hope not in three days'? Or was the stately figure in white a ghost who gave him the chilling answer: 'You will not exist beyond three days'? By midnight on the third day, he would die, he was told.

Ghost or dream, the story went round fashionable London with astonishing speed. For Lyttleton was so well-known. So infamous, in fact, that whatever he did was always a matter of interest and of gossip which outraged the more respectable members of society and which titillated and amused the rest. Lyttleton was the most profligate man of his age, a libertine exceptional for his excesses even in that most liberal of times. He was the 'wicked Lyttleton', a man steeped in the most fashionable vices of the age. Even members of his own family, shamed by his loose and prodigal behaviour, had long cut themselves off from him. Was it a wonder that they did so? Even as a member of the Tory government and a brilliant and persuasive speaker, he was regarded as a loose cannon and some feared that this scholarly young man might eventually in spite of all reach very high governmental office. How could they trust this dissolute fellow who had even deserted his wife and carted off a barmaid to live in Paris with him? Not that that was a long-term arrangement. As in all of his many affairs the woman was eventually thrown aside to fend for herself. Several women, some high-born, others from lower down the social scale, had cause to regret their association with Lyttleton, from which they usually emerged with no reputation and sometimes with no property.

More recently, Mrs Amphlett's three daughters, whom he had in turn seduced, had taken up with him on a more or less permanent basis. It is said that their mother died of a broken heart.

It was at his Hill Street home in Berkeley Square that Lyttleton had his experience on Thursday 24th November 1779. He described how he had heard a footstep at the bottom of his bed and when he looked up there was a figure all in white. She had pointed at him and uttered her awful warning.

It was a dream, he reassured his friends. At the same time there is some evidence that he took the matter seriously.

Lyttleton was an extremely superstitious man and such an experience shocked him. Nevertheless, he did his best to put it aside. On the next day he made a highly successful speech in the House on the condition of Ireland. That evening Hill Street was filled with guests. The usual roistering, dining, gambling took place until the early hours. The following day he met friends, laughed and joked with them about the dream or about the ghost, whichever way he chose to interpret it.

On the Saturday morning, the day before he was due to join his friend Andrews in Dartford, he told the Miss Amphletts who were staying with him: 'I have jockied the ghost as this is the third day'. He believed that he would 'bilk the ghost'. Later, walking through the graveyard of St James's church with his cousin Henry Fortescue, he pointed at the headstones. There was many a 'vulgar fellow' lying there, Lyttelton said, dead at his age, 35. 'But you and I who are gentlemen,' he announced confidently, 'shall live to a good old age.'

That afternoon Lyttleton left Hill Street for his country home, Pit Place, Epsom. Accompanying him were several friends including Fortescue, Captain Wolseley and the ladies described scornfully by Horace Walpole as both 'a caravan of nymphs' and 'four virgins of the Strand'. This hardly complimentary description of well-born ladies was meant to include two of the three Misses Amphlett, those regular camp-followers of his lordship.

Arrived at Pit Place, Lyttleton was taken ill. He had some kind of fit, of the sort that had frequently troubled him of late. He already had heart trouble and his health after years of dissipation was poor. Nevertheless, he recovered sufficiently to take a hearty dinner, 'supping plentifully on fish and venison.' It was a particularly rowdy occasion for many of Lyttleton's friends and hangers-on were invited, presumably to divert him from thoughts of midnight. He did himself express some confidence, saying to one of the Miss Amphletts that he did not expect to see any ghost that night. He went off to bed at 11.30, still a shade concerned perhaps that the third day was not yet over and that there was another 30 minutes left before he could breathe easily.

84

As Lyttleton prepared for bed he looked constantly at his watch. At 11.58 he called his manservant, William Stuckey, to close his bed curtains. But soon after midnight he was cheerfully asking about the bread rolls he would like for breakfast. Triumphant, he told the manservant: 'The mysterious lady is not a true prophetess, I find.'

Now Lord Lyttleton ordered the manservant to mix his medicine, a mixture of rhubarb and mint water, but was furious to see the man stirring it with a toothpick. 'Slovenly dog,' he shouted at Stuckey, telling him to bring a spoon. But when Stuckey returned to his master's bedroom only a minute or so later he saw that Lyttleton was seriously ill. Leaving the room once more he ran down to the drawing room where many of the guests were still enjoying themselves. 'My Lord is dying,' Stuckey called but by the time his friends arrived at his bedside Lyttleton was already dead. The watch he still held in his hand read 12.15. But the dead man had been deceived. He was unaware that his friends had advanced all of their watches by half an hour and that they had arranged for all of the clocks in the house to be similarly advanced. Even Lyttleton's own pocket watch and the clock by his bedside had been surreptitiously tampered with by his friends who had thought that they could in this way lessen his anxieties. And indeed it had done. But in keeping with the prophecy, his lordship died on the third day shortly before midnight.

This is one of the classic mysteries, involving two mysterious appearances, one *to* Lord Lyttleton, the other *of* Lord Lyttleton. Did a ghost really appear to Lyttleton? Or did he simply dream of the woman in white with her awful warning? Did he perhaps dwell on the promise of death? Did that cause heart failure? After all, it was said that he died young in years but old in body?

But what of Miles Andrews? What was it that he saw in his bedroom in Dartford at the very hour of his friend's death in Epsom? Whatever it was, it took Andrews three years to recover from the shock. He had no doubt that he had been visited by a man who had just died 30 miles away.

13

Time-Slips

Imagine ... you pass an acquaintance in the street and give a wave. Your acquaintance acknowledges you. He is going in the opposite direction. You immediately turn the corner and here is your acquaintance coming towards you once more. But he cannot be. That is impossible, for you saw him further back and going in the opposite direction only seconds earlier. He could not have arrived where he now is. To do that he would have had to turn back, run past you without your seeing him and then turn round and appear once more walking towards you. Or like some superhuman athlete he has raced round several streets to come face to face with you again. Or he has a double perhaps ... well, that is possible. He has a double though you never knew that. And remarkably, the double is only yards ahead of your acquaintance. Unless of course it is the double you are now seeing ... and isn't it strange that they are wearing identical clothes. And the second figure, now that he is up to you, also acknowledges your wave. No, this is without any doubt your friend.

There are several cases of this kind on record and it is reckoned that some kind of slippage in time has taken place. We imagine time to be something like a piece of string held out taut and that we move along it at the same pace. But, say this straight length of string somehow loses its tautness, that in some way it gets a loop in it. What if time sometimes does this? It may be a highly unscientific way of describing time but perhaps it helps us to understand what might have happened when you twice met your friend in the street. Either he or you somehow walked round the loop.

Enough of trying to describe time-slips. Here is a fascinating illustration from Tunbridge Wells. On the morning of 18th June 1968, an elderly lady, Mrs Charlotte Warburton, went shopping with her husband in the town. They decided to go their separate ways for a while and to meet up later. That morning, unable to find a particular brand of coffee from her usual grocer she went into a supermarket in Calverley Road. As she entered the shop she saw a small cafe through an entrance in the left-hand wall. She had never before realised that there was a cafe there. It was rather old-fashioned with wood panelled walls. There were no windows and the room was lit by a number of electric bulbs with frosted shades. There was at the time, she thought, nothing especially odd about the scene. 'Two women in rather long dresses were sitting at one table and about half a dozen men, all in dark lounge suits, were sitting at other tables further back in the room,' she said. 'All the people seemed to be drinking coffee and chatting ... a normal sight for a country town at 11 o'clock in the morning.'

Mrs Warburton did not stay but she certainly did not recognise anything amiss either then or indeed for several days. Even the rather formal and slightly off-key clothing made no immediate impression on her. Nor did the fact that although the customers were talking there was no noise from them cause her to question her senses. Nor did she notice that there was no smell of coffee.

There is clearly something strange here. Yet without questioning the circumstances in which she found herself, Mrs Warburton blithely left the cafe and went to meet her husband. And she did not suggest to him that the scene in the café seemed in any way odd.

When they came to Tunbridge Wells on their next shopping expedition Mrs Warburton decided to take her husband to the cafe. Or rather she hoped to take him there. But of course they never did find the place though they searched the street up and down. No, they were told in the supermarket, there was no cafe there. She must be in the wrong building. It was then that they learned about the Kosmos Kinema which had stood on the site of the supermarket. It had had a small cafe. They were directed to the Tunbridge Wells Constitutional Club where the steward told them that at one time the Constitutional Club had owned the premises adjoining the Kosmos which was now incorporated into the supermarket. The club had had an assembly room in those days and to the rear a small bar with tables for refreshments. Mrs Warburton's description tallied exactly with the club's old refreshment room.

The bar, the cinema and the assembly room had all vanished years ago, Mrs Warburton was told. Yet, on 18th June 1968, she had stepped into the past and like others involved in time-slips had accepted without question the place in which she found herself. Retrospective clairvoyance, it is called. Whatever it is, it is mighty odd to contemplate.

Another time-slip incident took place in Kent some years earlier. In 1935 Dr E.G. Moon, a very down-to-earth Scots physician with a practice in Broadstairs, was at Minster in Thanet visiting his patient, Lord Carson, who lived at Cleve Court, a haunted house referred to elsewhere in this book. After talking to Carson, the doctor left his patient and made his way downstairs into the hallway. His mind was clearly very occupied at the time with the instructions he had given the nurse about the prescription he had left for Carson. At the front door Dr Moon hesitated, wondering whether to go back upstairs to have another word with the nurse.

It was at this point that the doctor noted that his car was no longer where he had left it in the driveway. In fact, it had been parked alongside a thick yew hedge and that too was missing. Even the drive down which he had driven from the main road was now nothing but a muddy track, and a man was coming towards him.

The newcomer on the scene, only 30 yards from Dr Moon, was rather oddly dressed, wearing an old-fashioned coat with several capes around the shoulders. And he wore a top hat of the kind seen in the previous century. As he walked he smacked a switch against his riding boots. Over his shoulder he carried a long-barrelled gun. He stared hard at Moon. And the doctor registered the fact that the man coming towards him might have looked more at home in the 19th century.

Remarkably, Dr Moon seems not at the time to have been either alarmed or even mildly surprised by the changed scenery, by the quite oddly dressed man approaching him or the fact that his car was missing. What preoccupied him was the thought of Lord Carson's prescription. He simply turned away, without any concern, to go back into the house. But he did quite casually take one more look at the scene he was leaving. And now, as if by magic, the car was back where it had been and the yew hedge too. The drive was no longer a muddy track. And the man had also disappeared, back one assumes to the previous century. And it was only now that Dr Moon realised that something odd, something decidedly odd, had occurred.

All of this took seconds and so there is every reason to understand why Dr Moon did not immediately go out into the driveway to see where his missing car was. For the same reason it is understandable why he did not speak to the man dressed like a farm bailiff of the past. Dr Moon was drawn into some kind of accepting, hallucinatory state. When he came to – for that seems to be the best way of describing his return to his own time – he described to Lady Carson what he thought had occurred. He was anxious, however, that no word of it should come out in his lifetime for fear that his patients would begin to question his judgement. It was only after his death that the story was revealed.

It is difficult to grapple with the notion of time-slips. It may be that all past events are impressed into the fabric of buildings and that in some way and on some occasions they are released. In other words, what Mrs Warburton and Dr Moon saw were ghosts but not solely of people but of all of their surroundings.

Or did Mrs Warburton and Dr Moon actually return to a real, physical past? Did they turn up as strangers, were they really the interlopers, at somebody else's present? And if so – and this is an intriguing yet unanswerable question – did some people drinking coffee one Saturday morning in a Tunbridge Wells cafe look up and see Mrs Warburton? Did a man dressed like a farm bailiff, walking towards Cleve Court one day well over a hundred years earlier, see a strangely dressed doctor at the front door of the house? Did the coffee drinkers ever wonder where the elderly lady had so suddenly gone? And did the farm bailiff ask himself how the oddly dressed figure in the doorway had so suddenly disappeared?

Strangely, Tunbridge Wells has thrown up another odd story that may or not have been a time-slip. This tale goes back to some time in the mid-19th century and it took place in the Swan Hotel in The Pantiles. Mrs Nancy Fuller and her young daughter, Naomi, on a first visit to the town, took a room at the top of the hotel, the room now Number 16. As they climbed the stairs to their room the girl's behaviour began to change. She appeared more and more agitated, closing her eyes and whispering to herself. When her mother asked her what was wrong Naomi replied that she recognised the stairway, that she had been there before. Then she came out with the astounding remark that her lover was waiting for her in the room as he had said he always would. When they entered the room the young girl went at once to the corner, calling out 'John' as though to someone standing there waiting. For a few seconds in her mother's eyes she seemed to change, to grow older, and even her clothing was that of an earlier time.

The story that Naomi later told her mother was that she had previously lived in this building when it was a privately owned house. This was certainly before 1835 when it became The Swan. In the days when Naomi had lived there it had been known as High House. The young girl went on to explain that she had had a love affair with a man called John but her father had disapproved, had had the young man taken away and had locked her in the room. Alone in the room, aware that she would never again see him, she had conjured up the image of John and holding the hand of her imagined lover, she had jumped to her death from the window.

Room 16 is haunted. There are still tales of disarranged bed covers and of chairs being moved and tapping at the window.

Some have claimed to hear the cry 'John' carried on the wind.

But is this an early example of a time-slip? It differs from the other accounts in that Naomi was aware of a past life and her part in it. Some have regarded this story as an instance of reincarnation. Others have seen it as déja vu. But if reincarnation is the answer, what is it that triggers such an awareness of it? And if déja vu, how can that come about? It is all so complex. Perhaps it is simply a haunting resulting from a young girl's suicide. But the story is so curious that the idea of a time-slip is tempting.

14

Cranbrook's Pest House Ghost

Right from first seeing the house in early 1952 Robert Neumann, the Austrian psychologist, was strongly attracted to the place. As for Cranbrook, it was just what he believed old England must have looked like. With its wealth of old houses, Tudor and Jacobean, set in beautiful surrounding countryside, the village was idyllic. Steeped in its quintessential rural Englishness, unspoilt, peaceful, it was the ideal spot for contemplation, study, writing. And it had the advantage of being not too distant from London.

The Pest House in Frythe Walk had an ancient sagging roof which on one side came down almost to the ground. It had been built in 1369 as a one-room cottage and early in its existence it had been used as a pest house – that is, as a hospital in times of plague, small-pox and other infectious and contagious outbreaks. Later the house was extended for the priest and subsequent owners and then, in the 18th century, it was once more enlisted for use as a hospital. In the cellars, corpses from the plague years were buried. Ultimately the cellars were sealed up and it was finally converted into two separate houses.

In his book, *The Plague House Papers*, Robert Neumann acknowledges that on the day of his moving in, his cleaner told him that the couch in front of the fireplace was 'in the path'. She apparently knew the route the resident ghost sometimes took from the fireplace to other parts of the house. Furthermore, she told Neumann that she would not go up into the attics. They unnerved her. That same day the removal man was similarly reluctant to enter the low dark loft behind one of the attic 'guest rooms'.

Yet the two attic rooms were undeniably pleasant. From the window seats in the gable windows of the outer attic room there were extensive and beautiful views. The room itself, warm and extremely comfortable in daytime, cosy and intimate at night, had ancient floorboards and old rafters. Some recesses in the room had been walled off. The inner attic room was reached through this first room. And it was in there that it seemed to Neumann that some indefinable entity existed. It was as if there were some presence there which had seeped into the walls, a presence that sometimes oozed out. In this inner room were two old brick-walled cupboards of pre-Elizabethan date, which were in fact part of the chimney and fireplace immediately below which the cleaner had said was 'in the path'.

There certainly was an inexplicable uncanniness about The Pest House that made many visitors uncomfortable. There were noises. Dogs showed a marked reluctance to go into the attic and there was something about the place that caused a decided unease.

Some of Neumann's many visiting friends had disconcerting experiences while staying at The Pest House. A visiting American, for example, had asked one morning at breakfast who was the other lady staying in the house apart from its mistress and the housemaid. Was there another guest that he had been unaware of? Sleeping in the outer attic room, he had been disturbed by moans during the night. At first, in his sleepy state, he had thought that his wife was making the noise. He had wondered if she was unwell. As he struggled to full wakefulness, however, he became aware of a middle-aged lady, dressed in a sort of nightdress, passing his wife's bed. She seemed to be carrying an oil lamp. The American came to the conclusion that the woman was another guest he did not know about, sleeping, he assumed, in the inner attic room adjoining his. It did strike him as odd that Neumann had not mentioned that someone was sleeping in the next room. The American concluded that the woman was sick, which accounted for the moaning, and that she wished to go to the bathroom. As there were no toilet facilities in either attic room, anyone sleeping in the inner room who wished to use the bathroom in the night was obliged to pass through the outer room. To save the stranger any embarrassment, the American had feigned sleep until she had passed out of his room. He then lay awake for some time. He eventually fell asleep thinking that his surprise fellow guest was a long time returning to her room. Like several other guests, when the American couple came to realise who their night visitor had been, they cut short their stay.

But after one particular visitor had returned home from a stay at The Pest House, Neumann received a letter from her. And it was testy. She was not pleased with her host despite her pleasant stay at Cranbrook. On the last evening of her stay Davika – her surname is not known, only her unusual first name – had gone up to the attic room reserved for guests at The Pest House. She was a high-flying financial expert and she needed to dictate an urgent report on the national economic situation into her tape recorder.

Only when she returned to work in London the following day did Davika realise that her host had played such an infantile trick on her. Well, more than one trick really. She had not so much minded the nocturnal visitor to her room in the attic, she wrote. She thought that was some kind of practical joke. But the business with the tape recorder, this interfering with her serious research work, was really too much and not the sort of trick to be played on a guest.

'The only trick I cannot explain is the one you played with my tape recorder,' she wrote to Neumann. 'I only noticed it when the secretary brought me the typed text. I remember, of course, that halfway through the sentence about the progressive export quota I stopped to think for half a minute while the tape ran on, but when exactly did you play it back to find the empty spot? I thought I never lost sight of the machine. Also, if you absolutely must take advantage of other people's empty spots on their tape recorders, I should have hoped you would have been more witty. Dissembled voice and ancient English – well and good. But what is the meaning of "Eight pounds, oh, oh, eight pounds"... ? It was a somewhat silly joke.'

Certainly Davika was less concerned about the lady who had come into her room at 2 am. As she said, she could more or less work out how Neumann had done that. By the light of the moon she had seen the plump outline of a middle-aged lady come from the corner of the room where there was a locked door leading to a staircase beyond. The woman appeared to be wearing a night garment of some kind and, after looking down at Davika for some seconds she had left, shaking her head and moaning. She then gave the impression of walking through the closed door into the adjoining attic room. Davika was prepared to accept Neumann's tomfoolery, his setting up of this not terribly elaborate hoax, but she was unforgiving of his interfering with the tape recorder. She had not thought that her host would have dreamt of interfering with that.

And what was the meaning of the words – 'Eight pounds, oh, oh, eight pounds' – that Davika had found inserted into the text of the tape recorder in a 'dissembled voice and ancient English'? These words, in the 30-second vacant spot where she had paused in her dictation, were so inexplicable. What on earth had Neumann meant, Davika asked in her irritable letter.

In his reply to his guest Neumann was able to explain the figure which had passed through Davika's bedroom. That was no elaborate hoax, he told her. He admitted to The Pest House ghost, who was absolutely harmless. He knew that some of his guests might be disturbed at the thought of sleeping in a haunted room and so usually he did not tell them.

Nevertheless, Neumann had to confess to Davika that he had no idea of the ghost's identity. He was, however, particularly intrigued by her mention of the curious words on the tape recorder. What could be the significance of the words: 'Eight pounds, oh, oh, eight pounds'? And who could have uttered them? Could his ghost have been tape recorded?

It was a local historian who brought Neumann the clues he

needed to solve the mystery of The Pest House. An old document of 1578 revealed that some years earlier the governors of the local grammar school bought the property for use as a school 'with three Plague House Fields from Master Benenden and his daughter for an unknown sum.' Michael Benenden, who had sold the house for the not insubstantial sum of £44, insisted on the inclusion of 'an annuity for the unmarried daughter of the said seller, who shall also have the use of the house, during her natural life.' Five years later, her father now dead, Theresa Benenden's £8 annuity stopped. Doubtless at the time the agreement was made, some of the governors had had the idea that she would not live long for she was already middle-aged. Her confounding of the estimate regarding her life-span was costing them money. After all, £8 was not at that time a sum to be sniffed at. But Theresa Benenden's petition to the Queen to have the annuity honoured was rejected. Distraught, the wretched woman hanged herself in the cellar of The Pest House.

Thereafter, over the centuries, the portly figure of Theresa Benenden appeared at the house in which she had lived, had been defrauded and had died. Always garbed in some kind of night gown, she would walk across the large ground floor room, passing through a door without opening it, and then go on to the dining room. This was her regular path, beginning in the area of the fireplace, as the cleaner had informed Neumann. From the dining room she would pass through another door into a cupboard under the winding stairs. The entrance to the cellar was possibly in this part of the house. From this cupboard she, in Neumann's words, 'oozed up' to the first floor and thence to the attic. Here she passed through the narrow Victorian bedroom and into the second attic. In here she entered the built-in cupboard and thence passed through yet another wall into the upper part of the chimney.

An account of the haunting of The Pest House, written in 1801, suggests that Theresa's punishment, presumably for her having committed suicide, was to walk for 200 years. Her ghost was also, one assumes, to act as a reminder to those who had reneged on the financial arrangement. The especially wild years were from 1774 till 1779 when her ghost was said to have been laid. Carvings on the door of the dining room have caused some interest. They read: 'TB 1774, TB 1775, TB 1776, TB 1777, TB 1778'. Under these was a shape that looked like the figure 8 on its side. What does it all mean? Is TB Theresa Benenden? Are the dates to mark the last five years of her 200 year penance? And the figure 8 on its side... infinity? Eight pounds? Was her phantom not laid in 1778? Or was she laid temporarily, emerging once again when Neumann began renovations to the house and opening up the old cellars where she had committed suicide?

And what about that message on the tape recorder? What about the 'dissembled voice and ancient English', the words 'eight pounds, oh, oh, eight pounds'? Was that Theresa still bewailing the loss of her annuity, was that her speaking across a void to the 20th century? It does seem so.

15

Dover Castle's Ancient Mysteries

The guides who conduct visitors on tours around stately homes, great cathedrals and old castles are no different from the rest of us. They like the people they are dealing with to show interest. They like their tour parties to express some enthusiasm for what they have seen and to comment on the worthwhile nature of their visit. That's what makes it all worth doing. So at Dover Castle a few years ago the guides showed suitable appreciation at the gushing responses of the two Americans who had wandered round the castle and underground tunnels unaccompanied. Everything had been so well organised, they breathed, everything so realistic, so authentic. And they were particularly congratulatory about the sound system, especially in the area of St John's Tower. The groans and shrieks they had heard, why, at first they thought they were real. Wait till they told the folks back home, they said, smiling their way out.

Sensible of the guides to whom they spoke not to mention that there was no sound system in the specific area they were referring to. After the Americans had gone, and just to make sure, the guides checked to see if some visitor had fallen down and, unable to get up, had called out for help. Or perhaps someone was lost. But, no, there was no member of the public who had broken a leg or contrived to lose himself. So those groans and shrieks, well...

But in addition to noises off, Dover's great castle is home to several apparitions. It is hardly surprising that the place has over the past eight centuries absorbed so much of what the researchers Randles and Hough have called 'psychical residue', all the lingering waste emotion of past residents, their deepest hurts, their profoundest rages, hates and fears. Indeeed, right from the start, from those first days of its building in the 12th century, it was marked by cruelty and terror. Superstitious builders, worried that their work was being impeded by spirits, buried a dog in the walls and when its owner, an old woman, objected to the sacrifice, she was immured alongside the animal. Though the ghosts of the pair of them, the old woman and her dog, have not now been seen for 600 years, that is where it all begins.

In our time other apparitions from a long ago past have been spotted. In the Keep there is a man dressed in mid-17th century fashion, sporting a broad brimmed hat with a plume, a purple cloak and knee boots. A guide has seen a woman in a long red dress in the same part of the Keep. Then there is the Drummer Boy, murdered in the castle, they say, during the Napoleonic Wars, and who makes an appearance from time to time. In other parts of the castle a figure in blue has been seen and once the lower part of a man's body walked through the doorway of the King's Bedroom but when staff followed him into the room there was no one to be seen. Elsewhere, in the old Roman lighthouse there are claims that, very appropriately, a Roman soldier appears. In the Underground Works alias Hellfire Corner, that great warren of passageways, three miles in all, cut out by the military in wars against Napoleon and Hitler, a pikeman, garbed in 17th century style, has been seen to walk through the guardroom wall into the adjoining room.

Several of the guides have had recent interesting experiences. One day in 1992 Leslie Simpson was accompanying a group of 20 through the tunnels. He paused to play a recorded commentary but noticed that one of the party, a woman, was taking little interest in what was being said. Her attention was focused on something else. Suddenly, it appeared to Simpson that she was looking alarmed and as he went over to her she stumbled, going down on one knee. The guide's first impression was that she was ill. But, no, she was not ill though plainly shaken.

Hesitantly, she explained to Simpson that during the recorded commentary she noticed a man in naval uniform by a piece of machinery at the other end of the room. She imagined that he was a member of staff doing a repair. Then, she told the guide, the sailor had stood up and walked at speed towards the group. And it was then that she realised that this was no ordinary sailor for he walked through the barrier and then he had *walked through her*. At that point she had turned and lost her footing, going down on one knee.

Later in the day, Leslie Simpson had another group to guide around the tunnels. He decided to make sure that all was well and to check the area in advance. He went down to where the woman had earlier seen the apparition. There was no one there. But the door to an annexe, always shut, was open. From inside he heard an odd noise, best described as part-mechanical and part-animal. It was frightening. But then it stopped. Leslie Simpson has not heard it since and nor has anyone else. But the apparition of the naval man near the equipment was later seen by an Italian visitor.

Another guide, Karen Mennie, touring the tunnels with a party of visitors, reported a similarly curious happening in 1993. A man and his daughter appeared to be conversing quite seriously with an unseen third person. How bizarre this was and how even more bizarre when the father suddenly went away from the rest of the party. Later, when the tour was over, the father and daughter explained to Karen that they now realised that they had been speaking to a ghost. This is in itself remarkable for ghosts speak extremely rarely. At the time of the conversation the father and daughter had had no idea that they were speaking to a ghost. But then the ghost had given some important information about himself. He had been killed, he told his listeners, assembling an amplifier rack. The ghost had also told them that he had been a Postal Telecommunications Officer in Canterbury and that his name was Bill Billings. It was at that point that the ghost had disappeared and the father had tried to follow him. Karen Mennie had been disinclined to believe the story but to have two people swearing to have met a ghost half-convinced her that they were not deliberately lying. Perhaps they had been hallucinating. But is it likely that two hallucinate the same tale? And the name Bill Billings? The father and daughter seemed to think that he had been there during the war but records of that time are incomplete.

But did this Bill Billings ghost crop up again in 1994, shortly after the filming at Dover Castle of *Strange but True*, an LWT television programme presented by Michael Aspel? The producers introduced a psychic to see if he could detect any of the several ghostly figures associated with the buildings. He could not but he did say that the name 'Helen' kept coming into his head though neither he nor anyone else could say why. Some days after shooting was complete the assistant manager of the castle rang LWT. He wished to speak to one of the production team. An Australian tourist had met a very agitated ghost who kept repeating the name 'Helen'. Perhaps this was Bill Billings again. As for the Australian, he could not possibly have known about the psychic and the name which kept popping into his head. He was newly arrived in the country and the programme had not yet been broadcast.

Prior to the LWT programme, there had been two joint investigations of the phenomena at the castle by the Thanet Psychic and Paranormal Research Unit and the Association for the Scientific Study of Anomalous Phenomena. These were conducted in 1991, the first on 12th October and the second on 30th November.

Each time the investigators took with them all of the equipment now seen as essential to successful 'ghosthunting'. The teams were divided into eight pairs who were stationed at various strategic points around the castle and the underground to monitor whatever was to occur. Various items of sophisticated equipment – video and still cameras, tape recorders, thermometers – were positioned on stairways, near doorways, in passages. Then the investigators waited.

On the first occasion, on 12th October, a heavy wooden door

banged shut at precisely 11.22 pm. Nothing of note happened for another three hours and then, at 2.20 am there was another crash, this time behind locked wooden doors on the second floor. Adrian and Mary Coombs-Hoar who were stationed in that area at once unlocked the doors but they could see nothing which could account for the noise. But no sooner were the doors locked than they were shaken vigorously for several seconds. Adrian said: 'We both jumped out of our skins, petrified, then went back to the door which was vibrating madly.' Then, just as suddenly as it had begun, the vibrating of the doors came to a stop.

At the same time, two other team members posted in St John's Tower spotted a shadowy figure moving down the stone stairwell. One of them called out and the figure retreated back up the stairs. They were uncertain. Was it a colleague, they wondered. But when they questioned the only possible person it could have been, he told them that he had not been in that part of the building at the time they were speaking of.

At 3.30 am and 4.40 am the same pair of observers heard the banging of a heavy door. These sounds were tape recorded. No team members had been responsible for these noises. They had not been charging round the building slamming doors. Yet several of them heard similar noises in different parts of the buildings.

Back to the doors which the Coombs-Hoars had seen shaking so manically. The investigators had now trained a video camera on them. At 5.20 am, the doors again shuddered violently and there are six seconds of video tape which show this. Nor was there anyone on the other side of the door. The precautions taken by the investigators against the unlikely possibility of an over-enthusiastic team member ensured that fraud was impossible. In any event, no one could have had the strength to shake the doors so powerfully.

It was a remarkable few seconds for the witnesses. Chris Cherry who had put the camera in position was excited by what was happening before his eyes. He knew that he was in the presence of a powerful force of some kind. 'The noise was quite tremendous', he said, 'and all the tapestries above our heads started swaying.' In his excitement, Cherry shouted out: 'We've got it' and at once the manifestation came to a stop.

At the same time elsewhere in St John's Tower a noise described as 'enormous' quite overwhelmed four other investigators. One of them, Ian Peters, claimed that it did not so much frighten him as startle him out of his wits!

The watch on 30th November was less eventful. The most noteworthy occurrence took place in the Mural Gallery in the Keep. Here the tape recorder was switched off and later the sound of it being tampered with is recorded. Was this an intelligence at work or was some highly charged electrical energy present? And what was the reason for the strong smell of perfume in this part of the castle? Later during that vigil there were two loud crashes in the basement of the Keep.

Of course not everyone accepts that Dover Castle is haunted. Imagination, they say. It's the wind high up here, the air currents, the shadows. It's all capable of rational explanation. But is it? The scientists have provided first class equipment to record the odd events in this ancient place. The investigators have so organised themselves that cheating is virtually impossible. No, Dover Castle is imbued with its history; it is steeped in a past which is in the air, in the ether, in the walls. And that past comes out at times and impinges on those who care to visit. For several centuries this formidable stronghold was a centre of the utmost grandeur and power; it was also the scene of plotting, of torture, of murder and war. It is not surprising that it has its ghosts for within its walls have been enacted the most appalling crimes. It has been a place of the utmost sadness and desperation. Such places have their 'psychical residue'.

16

Strange Burials

Some people are born with such advantages that it is difficult not to feel the occasional pang of envy at their fine homes, their evident riches, the apparent ease with which their lives are conducted. They seem not to have to face the minor encumbrances of life. How fortunate they are! And yet experience reminds us that even those with the greatest advantages are, like the rest of us, prey to anxieties, beset by the devils of everyday life. So at St Michael's church at Cuxton in 1779, Margaret Coosens had herself buried in a small chamber with a glass door, enclosed inside a grey marble pyramid. The door was locked but inside was a key so that Mrs Coosens, dressed in red satin, could, were she to awake, were she to have been buried whilst in some kind of trance, let herself out and return to the living. It reminds one of the Gothic tale, *A Premature Burial*, by Edgar Allen Poe. As it was, Mrs Coosens, once inside, never emerged from her coffin.

Ann West of the old Bayhall Manor at Pembury was prey to similar fears and anxieties when she came to think of death. What if ...? she sometimes wondered. What if... ?

If there ever was an appropriate place for ghosts it is the derelict Bayhall Manor. Little of the magnificent old house remains now. The six foot thick outer walls are fallen and indeed for the last hundred or so years it has been deserted, its moss covered roofs collapsed, its massive doors no longer on their hinges, the window frames rotted. So much for the once extensive and powerful medieval fortified house and the later grand Jacobean mansion, hidden away and reached by steep and overgrown pathways through hop gardens.

Set in a secluded hollow, the decaying old house had a reputation even before the ghosthunters at the end of the 19th century decided to investigate what locals had described as groans coming from the house. Then a group of stout Tunbridge Wells gentlemen, armed with sticks, and perhaps really out for a lark rather than in the interests of scientific investigation, made their way in the dusk to the grim buildings. And they waited outside just for a moment to gather their courage. Then came a rumbling sound from inside the house. It was as if a body were being drawn across the floor. Impossible. The men laughed at the thought. At least some of them did. Others decided they had done quite enough for one night and began, with decent haste, to make their way back home. Other more intrepid souls were not to be put off so easily but after entering the house they heard the most unnerving thuds from the cellar and the most terrible groans. Like other groups who had dared face the perils of Bayhall Manor they too left very quickly.

It is supposed to be the ghost of Ann West who so troubles the house, the same Ann West who haunts Pembury churchyard where her table tomb reads:

To the Memory of
Mrs Ann West, late of Bayhall
In this Parish, who Died April 13th, 1803
Aged 34 Years

Poor terrified soul, she had not feared death so much as premature burial, the fear being of some kind of catatonic trance which would lead the doctor into believing her dead. And then, when she came round, she would find herself in the dark, in a coffin, deep in the ground and none would hear her calls. For days she would lie there, scratching, scratching, scratching at the coffin's lid and shrieking, shrieking, shrieking into the emptiness till finally, her voice gone, her nails torn, her finger ends bloodied, she would wait in terror for the end. The thought horrified her and on her last days as she lay ill in lonely Bayhall, such terrible imaginings possessed her unendingly.

Ann West summoned her lawyer, asking him to insert a new clause in her will. She was to be buried at Pembury Old Church in a coffin with the lid unscrewed and one end open. The lid was also to have a small window inserted. This was to be placed in a table tomb in the churchyard. At the east end of the tomb was to be inserted an iron-barred grille so fashioned that it could be opened from the inside.

Arrangements were also made for her bailiff to come to the tomb each evening at sunset with food and a flask of wine so that if Mrs West awoke suddenly from her trance she would be able to get up strength and prepare herself to meet the world once more. The bailiff was asked to continue his task for a year after the death of his mistress.

Alas for human promises. After Mrs West's death, the bailiff continued in his task for no more than a month. Presumably he gave it all up as a bad job. He had no expectation of the woman's resurrection and so upped and left for Australia. Rotten sort of fellow, anyway, for they say that he had robbed her for years and that his last actions were entirely in keeping with his previous behaviour.

So Ann West roams the lonely churchyard as well as Bayhall Manor. Did she really starve to death? Did she really lie there in the coffin's dark, calling, shouting, shrieking and at the end, whimpering? Did she starve after her bailiff deserted her? Was she unable to open the coffin lid or get to the grille?

Fifty years or so ago, the experienced ghosthunter Frederick Sanders paid a night-time visit to the churchyard. He peered inside the grille but all that he could make out by the beam of his torch was the skull lying on the floor of the tomb. The lower jaw was missing. He could make out nothing else. And that night no ghost walked.

A mile south-east of Lamberhurst is the 19th century Scotney Castle and near it the weather-stained tower of the old castle built in 1378. Nearby is the ruined Tudor manor house with its moat of water lilies. It is here that a most curious burial took place. Did

Arthur Darell fake his burial? And does the bedraggled form of a drowned man, said to stagger from the moat, have anything to do with Darell? Who is this who grips the edge of the moat and hauls himself up, the water running from him? Who is it who then makes his way to the great front door, pounding it with his fists till it is opened? And when the door is opened, why is there no one there on the step?

Arthur Darell inherited Scotney Castle from his brother and he died ten years later in 1710. A remarkable and scarcely believable tale is told about his funeral. As the coffin was being lowered into the grave a tall stranger in a long black cloak observed to another mourner: 'That is me they think they are burying.' After this he was not seen again. It is rather a tall tale to swallow. If a man were faking his own funeral it is unlikely that he would attend, much less pass such a strange comment. And it would be extremely difficult to effect a disguise good enough to deceive relatives and friends on such an occasion.

Yet over a hundred years later, John Bailey, the sexton, found Arthur Darell's massive iron-studded coffin in the Scotney Chapel in Lamberhurst church. When he raised the lid he saw only heavy stones. Was there something near the truth in the remark that the stranger in the cloak made at the funeral all those years earlier?

Stories are told of how Arthur Darell, having come into the inheritance, was constantly plagued by his four disagreeable and litigious sisters. They resented his ownership of the property. In consequence he sought a rather extravagant manner of escape. After his presumed death Scotney passed not to the sisters but to a kinsman. The sisters did not relent, however, and pursued a series of costly lawsuits against the new owner which led to the ultimate break-up of the estate.

A further extravagant twist to the story of Arthur Darell tells how, released from the constant harrying of his sisters, he now became involved in the smuggling trade. This may be believable enough but it is difficult to accept that he continued to use the grounds and the inner underground passageways of Scotney without being detected by others in the household. Still, Darell is said to have murdered a Revenue man by throwing him in the moat at Scotney. It is he, the murdered man, who emerges from the moat and who staggers across to hammer on the front door. At least that is one way of accounting for the phantom.

Yet there is another candidate for the identity of the drowned man at Scotney. This is the ghost of a man who did not die in the moat but whose adventurous escape from the house is recorded somehow in the very atmosphere of the place. It may be that, like an extract from an old film, the escape of Father Blount is played over and over again in the grounds of Scotney Castle. And it may be said that he too had undergone a kind of burial in the depths of the house when his enemies searched for him.

Father Richard Blount was a Jesuit missionary who lived in secret at Scotney, a sound and loyal Catholic house, from 1591. These were the years when Catholicism was anathema, when it was regarded as a dangerous creed, and when its priests were seen as a fifth column operating on behalf of Spain to bring about the downfall of Elizabeth I and her Protestant state. Yet the faith still had firm adherents, the rich among them willing to risk death at the stake to support and succour priests like Father Blount who had been smuggled into his own country, England, from Spain.

For seven years Blount worked from Scotney Castle, sometimes moving about the country to meet and sustain other Catholics and to conduct services in secret; at other times to discuss matters with emissaries from other European countries. But it was a precarious existence for the priest, as it was for members of the Darell family and their servants. Blount's hiding place was reached from a passageway under the stairs of the old Tudor house. Here he had two small rooms from which he could escape via a chimney which took him down to the ground floor. There was also a sloping shaft which led to a tiny stone chamber, cramped and dark, and this too served as an alternative hiding place.

At Christmas 1598 the authorities were informed of Blount's presence in the house. It was searched rigorously twice in ten days but 'in another secret place digged in a thick stone wall' Blount went undetected even though the searchers took up permanent residence in the house. Only once did he come near to being caught. At a time when the house was being searched, Mrs Darell saw the end of a belt protruding into the passageway from the secret door. To warn the hunted man inside she had to raise her voice but she was overheard. The searchers, confident that the fugitive was somewhere inside the thick walls, began to batter down the outside wall. They were likely to have broken through to the secret passageway by nightfall but a severe storm obliged them to abandon their work. Blount was aware that he could no longer stay at Scotney and resolved to escape at once. One of the servants was drawn into what must have been a last-minute piece of planning. In the evening when the searchers were having supper, the servant burst into their room calling out that their horses were being stolen. While the searchers ran out to the stables, Blount let himself out of his hiding place, ran to the moat and swam across. He disappeared into the night, never to be taken.

Is this the man dripping water? Is this Father Blount? Here, after all, was a highly charged moment. Not only was Blount and his mission in danger but many friends, including the Darells and their servants, who over the years had supported and sustained him, were now equally endangered. And there was the wider web of Catholics, all over the country, who were also involved and who, if Blount were captured and subjected to torture, might be imperilled. So perhaps the intensity of the moment has left its mark, regenerated from time to time.

Strange burials these; odd ghosts, really; and perhaps one of the living leaving his mark on time.

17

Davington's Murderer in the House

Snowy is still about. The old murderer is still there in the house. He still makes his presence felt. Not every day, of course, but from time to time he lets the people in the house know that he is still there. Not in any powerfully dramatic way for that has never been his style. But just enough for those in the old farmhouse facing Davington church to recall him to mind from time to time. So he may close or open doors; he may tinker with the lights; he may be heard as he walks across the creaking floorboards but he does little else. And no one in the household ever takes it amiss that Snowy is always there, moseying about the place, just as he has done since the Hitchcocks first moved there in 1960, and in fact just as he seems to have done in this old timbered house for the past 400 or so years.

From their earliest days the Hitchcocks heard noises in the upstairs rooms, more frequently during the day than at night. There were unaccountable draughts of cold air. A knife went missing from the cutlery drawer only to be rediscovered days later. There was the time when he took Mrs Hitchcock's nail varnish from upstairs and restored it some weeks later on the downstairs mantelpiece. But such eccentric occurrences disturbed none of the family. Vincent Hitchcock was a celebrated bullfighter, billed in Spain as 'El Ingles', and such unaccountable happenings made little impression on him, and indeed his wife, a former journalist, had seen too much to be deeply concerned.

Even the young Hitchcocks had the same phlegmatic attitude to whatever it was that bumped and moved about the house.

One evening in 1961 the Hitchcocks, who had spoken in the course of the meal about the curious happenings in the house, were urged by their dinner guests to hold a seance at the dinner table. The party, which included the television and drama critic Herbert Kretzmer, cut out the letters of the alphabet and then placing their hands on a tumbler, allowed it to move in various directions across the table. Of course, they all entered into the fun of it though no one appears to have had any expectation of a serious outcome. But ouija boards have powers.

And there on the dining table, as the tumbler stopped in front of one letter and then another, words were actually spelled out. Though astounded, the once sceptical Hitchcocks wondered if they really could be receiving some kind of spirit message. And the story which slowly took shape, letter by letter, was even more remarkable. Its narrator claimed to have lived in Tudor times, during the reign of Henry VIII. More surprising was his claim to be a hired assassin who had come from London to kill the owner of the house, a man called Wilkinson. But the plan went awry. The intended victim escaped. It was the teller of the tale, the presence which the Hitchcocks came to call Snowy, who died in a fire in the house which he had ever since haunted.

It was during these early days, shortly after the seance, that Vincent Hitchcock, redecorating the sitting room, decided to remove some of the worm-eaten wood panelling. What surprised him was his discovery, once the panelling was taken away, of previously concealed bricks which were burned black. A day or so later, Mrs Hitchcock, who had volunteered to collect for the lifeboat appeal, was visited by the local organiser. He also happened to be a fire inspector. Taken to see the bricks he declared at once that the house had suffered a serious fire in the distant past. In fact, it appeared to have been rebuilt on burnt-out foundations.

Oddly, over the years there were fires in the house and Mrs Hitchcock was to say in 1966 that 'the fire appliances know the road so well that they can find their way by instinct'. On one occasion fire damage revealed what was described as a 'priest's hole' and here some bones were found. Were these Snowy's last remains? Unfortunately, they were never given scientific analysis.

Vincent Hitchcock was not really convinced about the existence of Snowy. Nevertheless, on one occasion when he was in the house alone, he was roused in the early hours by the sound of choking. He went downstairs to investigate what might have been a break-in but his labrador dog uncharacteristically refused to leave the bedroom. There was no intruder; the doors and windows were locked. Yet the deeply sceptical Hitchcock had to admit that he felt there was someone in the house that night.

Twice more the Hitchcocks agreed at the request of guests to make a ouija board. Both times the cut-out letters and a tumbler were employed. On the first of these occasions Snowy's language was uninhibited and despite the archaic spelling, its sentiment was as clear as its expression coarse. Strangely, too, in the middle of the session the radiogram started up, playing the centre track of a long-playing Spanish record. This was played over and over, the needle declining to move on to the next track.

In the final seance Snowy made some reference to Spain and was asked if he spoke Spanish. His reply was odd. 'Souls have no language' was spelt out on the dining table. But spelling-out is language so that Snowy's claim seems to be disputable. This time Snowy's message referred to a family who, he said, bred bulls in a particular region of Spain. Vincent Hitchcock knew of no such family but on his return to Spain he asked people in the area. But no one seemed to have heard of any bull-breeders of that name. Then a very old man remembered hearing of such a family. They had been spoken of in his youth. But they had been long gone, over a hundred years in fact.

Snowy still manifests himself in the old house at Davington, but he seems content not to impinge too much on his hosts' good nature. They have accepted each other and the Hitchcocks have not tried to contact him in years. They lead their lives; he leads his unseen existence. At one time he used to move things about.

But he does not bother with that sort of trick nowadays. He simply keeps himself to himself.

And it is worth recalling that he was a professional murderer. Yet he has never frightened any of the Hitchcock family. Except perhaps the dog.

18

Lost Reputations at Ightham Mote and Sissinghurst

They say the presence of Dame Dorothy Selby can still be felt at Ightham Mote, that inexpressibly beautiful, moated medieval house. There is here such an overwhelming sense of the past in its mottled outer walls, in its great banqueting hall, in its Jacobean drawing rooms, in its chapel and crypt, along its silent passageways and in the inner courtyard. And there always had been a chill in the area where workmen found, a hundred years ago now, a concealed door within the walls. They broke in and found a female skeleton. Dame Dorothy? Even today in the tower bedroom there is still an unexplained chill in the air no matter what the time of day. That's Dame Dorothy, we are told, the one who betrayed the Gunpowder Plot to her cousin Lord Mounteagle. Privy to the plotters' designs to blow up Parliament and indeed supportive of their aims, she nevertheless had no wish that her favourite cousin should die. So she penned the following lines. Or so some say.

'My Lord, out of the love I bear to some of your friends, I have a care of your preservation. Therefore I would advise you, as you tender your life, to devise some excuse to shift of your attendance at this Parliament: for God and man hath concurred to punish the wickedness of this time.

And think not slightly of this advertisement, but retire yourself into your county where you may expect the event in safety. For though there be no appearance of any stir, yet I say they shall receive a terrible blow this Parliament; and yet they shall not see who hurts them. This counsel is not to be condemned because it may do you good and can do you no harm; for the danger is passed as soon as you have burnt the letter. And I hope God will give you the grace to make good use of it, to whose holy protection I commend you.'

Well, from there, matters went from bad to worse. The plotters, among them Guy Fawkes, were betrayed, rounded up, questioned, tortured, made to confess and then hanged, drawn and quartered. Some, however, were never taken and escaped, dallying long enough, according to the story, to call in at Ightham Mote and to punish Dame Dorothy. They walled her up and since then she has been the source of the sense of brooding and from her presence has come the sudden falls in temperature experienced in different parts of the house.

But is that really so? Look in the church with its great monuments and there you will find her memorial. No mention there of her being walled up. 'She was a Dorcas', the tablet says: that is, she was famed for her good works. Furthermore, she was a fine needlewoman and on the back of her tomb are two representations of her famed needlework pictures. From here emanate the false charges and, indeed, the false legend associated with her. In fact, Dame Dorothy Selby is said to have bled to death after pricking her finger when at her tapestry.

The first picture on her tomb illustrates Adam and Eve in Eden. The second is an attempt to illustrate the Roman Catholic conspiracies against England: in the centre the Pope presides at a meeting at which these plots are hatched; then, on the left are the ships of the Armada; on the right are the cellars of Parliament with powder barrels covered with faggots and Guy Fawkes approaching with a lantern. Then comes the line from which the whole connection of Dorothy Selby with the plotters comes:

'Whose Arte disclosed that Plot, which had it taken, Rome had triumphed and Britain's walls had shaken'.

This line, misinterpreted, is the one which suggests her guilt and from it flows the story of the walling up.

But then, if it is not Dame Dorothy, who is it who haunts Ightham Mote? Difficult to say but there are candidates from a story dating back to 1552. At that time, for some reason or other, the legend has it that the then occupant of the Mote, Sir Thomas Browne, murdered a serving girl and hid the body inside the walls. Another version of the tale has the priest to Sir Thomas involved in a scandalous affair with a female servant. He apparently committed suicide and the girl was punished, presumably by Sir Thomas, by being bricked up. So perhaps the ghost of Ightham Mote is not Dame Dorothy Selby, one of Queen Elizabeth's waiting ladies, but rather an earlier much less exalted figure.

There is little doubt about the haunting but it does not seem right that Dame Dorothy, though she may be one of the ghosts, should be made to carry the burden of such a twisting of her life story. As in the case of Sir John Baker of Sissinghurst, a reputation takes a tumble. Was he the wicked and cruel persecutor whose ghost used to walk at Sissinghurst?

Baker's story has much of the fairy tale about it. He was known not just as a persecutor of Protestants in Mary Tudor's reign and called 'Bloody' Baker but he also came to be called 'the English Bluebeard'. And just as a reminder, here is the French Bluebeard...

'Once upon a time there was a man who owned splendid town and country houses, gold and silver plate, tapestries and coaches gilt all over. He had already married several wives and no one knew what had become of them. One day his latest wife was left alone in the house and given charge of the keys and in her curiosity she decided to open the door to the Forbidden Room. At first she saw nothing for the windows were closed but after a few moments she perceived dimly that the floor was entirely covered with clotted blood and that in this were reflected the dead bodies of several women that hung along the walls. These were all the wives of Bluebeard whose throats he had cut one after another.'

Well, that is the Bluebeard of the French writer, Charles Perrault. And we, it seems, had our own English Bluebeard, another mass murderer, so we are told, more or less along the lines of the French one. Sir John Baker may well be a Kent ghost but whether he deserves such a bad reputation is doubtful.

Still, they tell the tale in Kent of how one of Baker's betrothed decided to take her friend along with her to see the fine castle in which he lived at Sissinghurst. And when the friend saw the place in the distance, its long driveway and its fine gate house, its commanding turrets, its broad pitched roofs and towers, she could scarce contain her envy. And when she approached the wonderful gardens and the splendid walls and the massive oak door she was almost speechless at the good fortune of the young girl who was to be the wife of the owner of such a fine place. Then they pushed their way into the great hall with its beautiful furnishings from all over the world. And they gazed together in admiration at the splendour of it all when from behind them came a call, a fierce squawking, and as they turned, their eyes fell upon a parrot with a plumage of red and green and gold. And the parrot spoke to them thus:

'Peapot, pretty lady, be not bold
Or your blood will soon run cold.'

But they did not take notice of what they were told for they simply laughed at such a quaint message and they continued to peep here and pry there. And then they heard the master of the house approaching from outside, heard him turn the handle of the great door, heard his footsteps as he entered the hall.

'Let us hide for the sport of it,' Sir John's fiancee said. 'Let us give my loved one a surprise.' And so they hid in the stairwell and he came slowly closer and closer. As he came they saw that he carried something over his shoulder and as he drew yet closer it was plain that what he carried was a woman's body. Nor did he see them as he mounted the stair whilst the young women below held their breath. And when he was but a few steps from the top of the stairs one of the dead woman's fingers which had a heavy ring snagged on the banisters. So he took his dagger from his waistband and chopped it off. The finger, still with its ring in place, fell down the stairwell where the girls caught it, placed it in a neckerchief and when they could, they made their escape. They fled to the nearest town and alerted the mayor and the justices who went to make an arrest. The dead woman was recognised by the ring on her finger and the wicked Sir John Baker was caught and punished with death.

Thus the Bluebeard of Kent, Sir John Baker of Sissinghurst Castle. Hardly surprising that there is a ghost at this castle, considering such a monster of a man.

But such are reputations. Sir John Baker never really matched up to the story which came to be told about him. He was of course a significant political figure in Tudor England. He held positions of the highest rank being in turn a Member of Parliament, Attorney General, Chancellor and Speaker of the House of Commons. But it was his role in the diocese of Canterbury during the reign of Mary Tudor that most effectively earned him his reputation. He was commissioned by the Queen to hunt out heretics – Protestants – within the diocese of Canterbury. And as a Catholic and a servant of his Queen that is precisely what he did. Whilst he most certainly questioned some over their religious allegiances and signed many a death warrant, it is most unlikely that he personally participated in torturing anyone. It is said that in a little apartment over the south porch of the parish church, known as Baker's Hole, he abused those found guilty before having them burned at the stake. More likely he worked conscientiously according to his beliefs and held the view that what was being done was for the good of the country. And let us not forget that this was the 16th century.

Other stories abounded about this most hated man, stories which grew in the telling, year upon year. He was a lecher and rapist, it is said, a man who personally had slain a woman with his sword when she disobeyed him in some or other matter. And this was to be the basis of the Bluebeard tale as it attached to him.

Sir John Baker, by the way, contrary to the story, died in his bed at the age of 70. He might of course have been sent to the stake himself had he lived long enough. Fortunately for him, he died just as Queen Elizabeth came to the throne and before it was the turn of Catholics to be persecuted. One story has it that he was in his turn tortured and then burned in an iron cage which he had made for his own victims. Don't believe it.

Still, as you might expect, Baker's ghost used to walk the grounds of Sissinghurst. In more recent times a priest has been seen. But who is he? Was he walled up in the castle as some have said? Or is he a spirit anxious in some way to save the wicked soul of 'Bloody' Baker? Or does he seek revenge on that man?

Dame Dorothy and Sir John may well be among the best known ghosts of Kent but are the reputations they have been saddled with truly their own?

19

Phantoms at The Pantiles

The reason for concluding these accounts of supernatural and paranormal occurrences with a series of reports from a narrow area of Tunbridge Wells, just a few haunted acres, is not that the stories are especially thrilling. Indeed most of them are merely fragments, sketchy accounts, collected together by Geoff Butler who lives on The Pantiles, that elegant, shaded walk, that centuries-old centre of high fashion and the beau-monde.

It is not even that the stories are easily verifiable. They must be taken at their face value. But what does give them credence is the fact that they are all so matter of fact and that they are not rounded tales with a beginning, middle or end. They do not have about them the smack of invention; they have no breath of fiction about them. They are simply people's accounts of events of the briefest duration which to them are inexplicable. They are in fact so very similar to the countless reports of unaccountable incidents that are recorded in every year.

So to The Pantiles where articles go missing; temperatures change; objects are moved; dogs refuse to enter rooms; unusual smells linger on the air and there are unseen presences in rooms. And there are apparitions, too, some very obviously from times past and others so evidently from today.

Start with Grey Ladies. Over many years there have been reports of a matronly figure dressed in grey sitting at the first floor window of Binns Restaurant overlooking The Pantiles. She does not do much. She just sits. Another Grey Lady was spotted in the Swan Hotel on 2nd October 1997. Are we to assume that all ladies in the past wore grey? Or do many apparitions appear in a kind of monochrome? As a relief from ladies in grey, there is the lady in black at York Cottage. Several witnesses, including the present occupants, have reported her presence. She stands by the front gate and the general view is that she is happy. But she too appears to do nothing. It does not seem that there is an intelligence or feeling here in the way there seems to be with, say, the Grey Lady of Cleve Court or any of those manifestations requiring release or exorcism. It is as if a snatch of film is undergoing a constant repeat but there is no clear narrative. The Grey and Black Ladies of Tunbridge Wells seem like left-overs.

The figure seen by Daniella Bayfield, the owner of Master Transcriptions, is much the same. She is a young girl dressed in Georgian clothing who sits on the old milestone outside her building. Geoff Butler writes: 'She seems so much part of the scene that we wonder if the girl is waiting perhaps for her boyfriend – or is she waiting for the coach to London?' Like many other of the apparitions mentioned in this book – for example, those seen on Blue Bell Hill – she looks perfectly ordinary and solid. She is certainly not one of those who seem to be for ever on the wander as though searching for something. She can best be regarded as another accidental left-over, an echo of the past, perhaps, or a reflection, but not the sort of ghost who is in need of release. She is possibly best described as another example of 'psychical residue'.

A lady, who wishes to remain anonymous, lives in a flat in The Pantiles. One day during the summer of 1997 she began to feel uneasy in the house although she was unable to account for this. In the early hours of 5th August she woke and at once sensed that she was not alone. She got out of bed and then saw what she took at first to be her own reflection in the window. With a start she realised that it could not be for what she saw was a back view of a figure, dressed in modern clothing. The witness thinks that this shadowy visitor might then have been joined by another figure although she is uncertain of this. Whatever it was then disappeared, leaving her extremely distressed.

What is particularly intriguing is that in some way this

manifestation may be linked with other curious happenings in The Pantiles in the same week when there was a Georgian Festival in the town. How appropriate that the great watering place should celebrate its garish past, the times of the future George IV and all his louche companions, who on the Brighton, Bath, Cheltenham spa circuit, always had time for Tunbridge Wells with its Assembly Rooms, its Beau Nash, its card games, races, balls and, of course, its waters.

Modern festivals, those great outdoor theatres, naturally need changing rooms and administrative centres throughout the towns in which they are organised. So it was in Tunbridge Wells where an empty shop in The Pantiles – No 11 – happened to be available. It was here that Emma Heddon and Stephanie Wallis acted as wardrobe mistresses, charged during the Festival with caring for the performers' costumes. On the first night of the performance, 30th July, 1997, they found one item of costume, a reproduction Georgian riding skirt, on the floor. Well, that sort of thing happens. But the following night the skirt was on the floor again and this time an antique gun, another property item, lay on top of it. The girls made enquiries but no one claimed responsibility for moving either the skirt or the gun. There is no previous evidence of No 11 being haunted. A poltergeist? Perhaps.

What is of interest is the dates of these supernatural activities. Odd, isn't it, that in the same week there should be manifestations of two quite distinct kinds in Pantiles buildings relatively close to each other? Were there any particular conditions which might cause an outbreak of such activities? Many of the investigators into these matters are of the view that distinct meteorological features – high pressure, storm conditions – set some ghostly activities in train. Local weather conditions during high summer when it was extremely warm were possibly unusual enough to spark off poltergeists or other ghostly activities.

And is the following incident relevant? At about 6.30 one morning in May of the previous year, the local roadsweeper, Kenneth Morgan, was passing the building next to No 11, the one that was to be used as a changing room. During that period the building – Nos 9 to 15 The Pantiles – was undergoing renovations but there were no workmen about at that early hour. And that is why Mr Morgan's attention was drawn to the noise of heavy timbers being thrown about. As he looked through the window he saw the lumps of wood in motion as though they were being hurled about.

When the builders arrived later they found no sign of disturbance. Was some kind of apparition presenting itself to Kenneth Morgan? Or was it a poltergeist in action? It certainly sounds like poltergeist activity although they are usually not so prepared to tidy up after their activities. And if it was a poltergeist was it responsible for the disturbances experienced by the girls next door the following year?

Then there is the other nearby house – No 7 The Pantiles – to take into account. Spencer Ayres and Julia Millbank who moved in 1996 have reported that items in the house have been unaccountably moved. They also tell of the experience of James Simpson, their visitor, who lying in bed one night, sensed a presence in the corner of the bedroom. He felt himself to be physically powerless, unable to move. It was as though he was tied to his bed. This is similar to the experience of Eric Essex who in 1966 had been unable to speak or move until the mysterious presence moved off his bed in the house in Waterdales in Northfleet.

Julia Millbank has also experienced temperature changes, a common enough feature in matters supernatural. This is why the investigators at Dover Castle included thermometers in their equipment when they tried to track the manifestations there. There really does seem to be a powerfully active entity of some kind operating in these neighbouring houses.

Elsewhere in The Pantiles, there are accounts of a dog in No 23B refusing to go into a room, a reminder of the behaviour of Lady Carson's spaniel, Susan, at Cleve Court. Some years ago one occupant of this flat, Mrs Jo Morgan, reported that there had always been strange occurrences there. On three separate occasions, she said, the bedclothes were pulled from her daughter Samantha's bed. Despite putting up a struggle the bedding was each time wrenched from the girl's grasp with considerable force.

In Geoff Butler's house, No 48, there was an odd experience in 1978. A carpenter and an electrician were working together on building work in the cellar. On one occasion, after telling the carpenter, the electrician turned off the power supply. The carpenter, getting on with his work in the dark, went on chatting to his workmate. Only when the light was restored did he realise that he was on his own. The electrician had been on another floor. Yet the carpenter had been aware of a presence in the darkness of the cellar. Whose?

Did it have any link with two hauntings in 1980 at Nos 44 to 46, now a restaurant and bar called Springs but then, serving the same function, called The Chalet Arosa? An employee, David Lawrence, had just locked up when he thought he heard footsteps in the bar. When he reopened it, he saw a casually dressed man wearing a leather apron. As soon as he challenged the stranger, the figure vanished.

Some weeks later, the manager, Pat Humphreys, in bed in one of the upstairs flats, found that he could not sleep. There had been a dramatic fall in temperature and he felt extremely cold. Then, on the wall of his bedroom, he saw a light which grew, transformed its shape and then materialised into a man wearing a carpenter's apron. The figure moved across the room and passed through the wall.

Was it this workman the carpenter thought he was talking to in the cellar of 48? Was the figure seen by David Lawrence the same one as was seen by Pat Humphreys? Are we considering three different presences here? Or two? Or one?

The subsequent owners of the restaurant/bar never saw any apparition but they did claim that they were very often conscious of some indefinable presence in the kitchen and that on the stairs they felt at times that someone was trying to pass them.

And what is it that the owner of the post office at No 40 smells as he opens up the premises each morning? He claims it is pipe tobacco, just as the Friends of Chatham Theatre Royal think they smell tobacco in the auditorium of a building in which for many years there has been no smoking. Do smells have their own echoes? Is the smell in the post office anything to do with the fact that the building was at one time part of the Assembly Rooms or that there were coffee rooms nearby? Do some of the smells of the past's high living days linger on?

Then of course there are stories of the Common opposite The Pantiles. There is the black horse and its rider with his mauve cloak. There is the enormously fat female who is thought to be Mary Jennings, a notorious drunkard, 'built like a barrel', and who died in 1736. There is the young woman falling to her death from Wellington Rocks in 1917, heard by a witness to call out her lover's name. They say that even today, though she is never seen, her voice can be heard calling out 'Daniel'.

So many phantoms who leave us with many unanswered questions. But the major question is: Why are there so many ghosts in such a small area of an English country town? What is the secret of these few haunted acres?

Bibliography

Geoffrey Butler, *Pantiles Ghosts*, Privately published, 1996

Alan Bignell, *Kent Village Book*, Countryside Books, 1986

Joseph Braddock, *Haunted Houses*, Chivers, 1966

Manfred Cassirer, *The Persecution of Mr Tony Elms*, (Privately published) 1993

Marcus Crouch, *Discovering Kent*, Shire Books, 1975

Joan Forman, *The Haunted South*, Hale, 1978

Andrew Green, *Haunted Houses*, Shire Books, 1979

Andrew Green, *Our Haunted Kingdom*, Wolfe, 1973

Andrew Green, *Haunted Kent Today*, SB Publications, 1999

Andrew Green, *Ghosts of the South East*, David and Charles, 1976

Andrew Green, *Ghosts of Today*, Kaye and Ward, 1980

John E. Heymer, *The Entrancing Flame*, Little Brown, 1996

Peter Hough, *Supernatural Britain*, Chivers, 1995

R.H. Lewis, *Ghosts, Hauntings and the Supernatural World*, David and Charles, 1991

Andrew Mackenzie, *Hauntings and Apparitions*, Heinemann, 1982

Andrew Mackenzie, *A Gallery of Ghosts*, Barker, 1972

Robert Neumann, *The Plague House Papers*, Hutchinson, 1959

Brian Paine (ed) with Trevor Sturgess, *Unexplained Kent*, Breedon Books, 1997

Jenny Randles, *The Paranormal Source Book*, Piatkus, 1996

Jenny Randles and Peter Hough, *Strange But True?*, Piatkus, 1994

Jenny Randles and Peter Hough, *Spontaneous Human Combustion*, Hale, 1992

Frederick Sanders, *Psychical Research in Haunted Kent*, (Privately published) 1946

John and Anne Spencer, *The Ghost Handbook*, Boxtree, 1998

Peter Underwood, *This Haunted Isle*, Harrap, 1984

Peter Underwood, *Nights in Haunted Houses*, Headline, 1994

Peter Underwood, *Ghosts of Kent*, Meresborough, 1984

John E. Vigar, *Curious Kent*, Meresborough, 1984

Ian Wilson, *In Search of Ghosts*, 1995

Index